The IRRESPONSIBLE TRAVELLER
TALES OF SCRAPES AND NARROW ESCAPES

Compiled and edited by
Jennifer Barclay and **Adrian Phillips**

Bradt

Reprinted December 2014
First published in the UK in September 2014 by

Bradt Travel Guides Ltd
IDC House, The Vale, Chalfont St Peter, Bucks SL9 9RZ, England
www.bradtguides.com

Published in the USA by The Globe Pequot Press Inc,
PO Box 480, Guilford, Connecticut 06437-0480

Text copyright © 2014 Bradt Travel Guides Ltd

Edited by Jennifer Barclay and Adrian Phillips
Typesetting by Ian Spick
Cover design: illustration and concept by Neil Gower

ISBN: 978 1 84162 562 1

British Library Cataloguing in Publication Data
A catalogue record for this book is available from the British Library

Many thanks to Eland Publishing Ltd, The Orion Publishing Group and *The Spectator* for permission to
reproduce three extracts in this book.

'The Irresponsible Traveller' Trade Mark is owned by Nick Redmayne, who blogs at
theirresponsibletraveller.co.uk. While Nick has contributed a story, this book is unconnected
with that website.

Production managed by Jellyfish Print Solutions; printed in the UK

Contents

Introduction
by Hilary Bradt

The words 'Responsible Travel' are now familiar to us all and I'm proud to say that Bradt Travel Guides were at the forefront of the movement with an article in a national newspaper in 1992 and an emphasis on this aspect of travel in our guidebooks.

However, the truth is that when travel writers get together they tend not to talk about how well they've behaved or the latest eco initiatives. At least, those aren't the *first* things they talk about. The tales that come first are those of uncomfortable moments on the road, unpublishable stories of times when things went wrong, sometimes because of their own irresponsibility.

I remember one such conversation: drinks in hand, a group of us were batting around book ideas, getting sillier as the evening wore on, when Mike Unwin recounted his irresponsible and hilarious experience trying to smuggle hard currency out of Zimbabwe in a train toilet. A year or so later, Alex Robinson told me his spine-chilling tale of coming within a second of being murdered by bandits in Brazil, and I knew that the time was ripe for a collection of 'tales of scrapes and narrow escapes'.

The Irresponsible Traveller seemed the perfect publication to celebrate the 40th anniversary of the founding of Bradt Travel Guides. Most of the 40 contributors are professional writers and broadcasters. But we've also included a handful of new writers whose entries to the annual Bradt/*Independent on Sunday* Travel Writing Competition grabbed our attention. We will hear more from them in the future, we're very sure.

Travel is a process of learning what you don't know. And sometimes you have to learn the hard way.

Tim Cahill

A Stranger's Smile
Zoe Efstathiou

'I'll see you soon,' he says, squeezing my hand. In India, hand-squeezing has become our way of kissing in public. I should just go and catch my train but we've had such a nice day together. He quickly glances over his shoulder to see if anyone is looking and then leans forward and plants a kiss on my lips.

'See you soon,' I say finally, as I let go of his hand and swipe my token across the barrier of the Delhi metro station. He winks and walks away.

I am halfway down the escalator when I feel someone looking at me. I glance over my shoulder and my eyes meet with those of a man in his fifties or sixties standing behind me. I am wearing a vest top and a pashmina. Like a reflex, I adjust my pashmina to make sure my shoulders and chest are covered. I hear the man mutter something under his breath. He steps forward to stand right next to me and turns his head to face mine. He repeats the word, but I can't make it out. A slur in Hindi, probably.

His brown eyes are narrowed with a look of disdain. The skin around them is lined with dozens of fine wrinkles. I fiddle with the zip on my handbag. *Don't be intimidated*, I think. *Ignore him.* I look ahead, but I can see his face out of the corner of my eye, staring at me. *Ignore him*, I tell myself, but then I quickly glance over and see that yes, he is still staring at me. There is a black strap across his chest. I see that it holds a small, curved knife, kept in a red-painted holster at his hip. *What the hell?* I feel something burn through me, a flash of fear that quickly turns to anger. Anger at being intimidated for no reason, anger that a man at least thirty years older than me with a menacing little knife feels he has the right to come and stand next to me and mutter under his breath. *Who does he think he is?* I look right back at him. *You don't scare me,* I think, and we stare at each other until the escalator reaches the ground floor. I look away and smile to myself just to make it clear that he has had no effect on me. I walk to my platform, not bothering to look back.

I check my watch while I wait for the train. It's 10.15 p.m. The hotel I'm staying at has an 11 p.m. curfew but it's only three metro stops away. I watch the train approaching and then see him, the man with the angry eyes, walk on to the platform, his hands in his pockets, glaring at me.

We both get on to the train through doors a few metres apart. Keen to get away from him, I walk through at least six carriages. I eventually stop and pretend to study the train map above the carriage doors before glancing back, only to see him standing further down the carriage, staring at me. The knife seems bigger than before and the carriage is empty. I feel the electric mix of fear and anger, and march down the train as it leaves the platform and starts pulsing through the veins of the underground.

Why is this train so empty? I wonder, panicking. I glance over my shoulder and see him striding after me. He is no longer looking at me and wears a blasé expression as if what he is doing is completely normal and non-threatening. *What does he do with that knife?* I imagine him cornering me, dragging the curved blade across my face. *Oh God. Oh God,* I plead, as I approach the end of the train. *Where do I go now?*

An automated woman's voice is saying something. I realise she is announcing our arrival at the next stop. The train pulls into the station and I leap off and practically run down the deserted platform. I look back and see him walking briskly after me, his knife flapping at his side.

I jump back on to the train to confuse him but he follows. He is standing at the end of the carriage and casually loops his hand into an overhead handle. He looks right at me.

The doors begin to close. My heart is racing. I make a dash for it and throw myself through the narrowing gap. I scan the platform. He's not there. The doors are closed. The train is pulling away. And then through the window I see him and he smiles.

Zoe Efstathiou is an NCTJ-trained journalist who writes freelance travel and beauty features. This story was shortlisted for the Bradt/*Independent on Sunday* Travel Writing Competition in 2012. Despite her scary encounter on the Delhi metro, Zoe visits India as often as possible, finding her experiences there a great source of inspiration.

The Ups and Downs of Bhutan

Ben Ross

It's very dark now, and there's a ripe tang of diesel and pine cone in the air. I give my bicycle brakes another squeeze then spill forward into the night, a moth in the headlights of the oncoming trucks. Another of these monsters grinds up towards me, part of a dotted line of rush-hour traffic edging along the mountainside. It passes in a clattering roar, squeezing me to the road edge. To my left lies only blackness, a sheer drop to the valley floor perhaps, or a neck broken on invisible trees. Either way, oblivion is at my elbow, just a misjudged pot-hole away. And there are many of these to be misjudged.

I should stop. I should wait. Death or injury is a genuine possibility – and I don't even know the name of the town I'm freewheeling towards. Even if I make it there intact, I might miss it in the rush, carry on this mad spiral for hours more through the night. But for some reason – and I can't explain it, I know it's not rational – I just speed on downwards, through fizzing nocturnal insects and dust. Another hairpin bend, and I still haven't got the hang of these brakes. It's a jolting, only-just-in-control manoeuvre. Head on, another HGV rises: bright, white light in the void. That smell of diesel again, the blue smoke of the thunder dragon.

Thunder dragons. They're all over the place around here, but usually of a more mythical, tourist-friendly variety. Bhutan is Druk Yul, Land of the Thunder Dragon, and travel brochures for the country regularly call on a mythology made up of unlikely creatures performing astounding feats. I'd already climbed breathlessly up to the Taktsang monastery – Bhutan's best-known site – an impossible building plonked halfway up a cliff face in what appears to be a one-fingered rebuke to gravity, elderly hikers and sensible planning laws. It's commonly known as Tiger's Nest, because a Buddhist master called Guru Rinpoche is reputed to have flown there on the back of a tigress to subdue evil spirits. Raise an eyebrow at the local Buddhists and they're likely to nod energetically. It's all real, they insist: a dash of legendary colour on the long road to enlightenment.

Non-legendary, modern-day Bhutan is exuberant in a different sort of way. 'Gross National Happiness' is its ongoing mantra, revealed on government posters and rhapsodised at length by tour guides. This tiny Himalayan outpost, just twice the size of Wales, may be perched between two fire-breathing economies – China to the north, India to the south – but the spiritual calm of the populace counts for more, apparently, than the rush of inward investment that might mend these craters in the tarmac, or provide a few crash barriers.

Back in 1972, the then-king Jigme Singye Wangchuck pronounced that economic progress had to be managed according to the country's Buddhist principles, and since then nothing has happened in any great rush. Television arrived only in 1999; the mobile phone network is box fresh. So, a big yes to subsistence farming (crops harvested by hand, cattle pulling the ploughs) and no thank you very much to unsustainable development, billboard advertising and – refreshingly – cigarette-smoking. Visitors are encouraged, but they still number only in the tens of thousands annually. Even with a chunky daily tourism tax, that doesn't raise the sort of money needed to create the infrastructure that will stop me wrapping myself round a tree trunk.

Did I mention that I don't have any lights? Or reflective gear? The whole moth idea is more strategy than analogy. I'm using the beams from the oncoming trucks as a guide for where I should be going.

When there's a gap in the traffic I can see almost nothing: dark blues on blacks. Somewhere below me is Chris, another – faster – journalist, who'd coaxed me patiently up the mountain in the afternoon. And far beyond him, no doubt, will be the Australian, a technology addict who's imported his own heavily sprung bike especially for this trip and has festooned himself with onboard tachometers and video gear. He's presumably made it to the bottom already and will even now be uploading a greatest hits compilation of skids and wheelies via his Bluetooth headcam. To me, the Australian appears slightly deranged. Earlier, he'd decided to cycle up the hundreds of steps that lead to Tiger's Nest, occasionally pausing to film himself doing it. It appeared rather sacrilegious, but the Buddhists didn't seem to mind.

My approach to cycling is somewhat different from his, and can be summarised thus: flat is best. At home, I potter to work and back on my ageing Ridgeback Cyclone, but I don't pretend to get a kick out of it. Nor can I demonstrate any zen in the art of pedal-cycle maintenance. It takes a good few weeks of the gears jamming in ever-more outrageous ways before I'm prepared to run the gauntlet of a bike shop, where I tend to be patronised and ripped off in equal measure. I choose quiet roads and parks for my commute, part of an almost Bhutanese desire to embrace serenity and avoid the violent maelstrom of London's major roads.

In this and, I'm sure, in many other things, Jigme Khesar Namgyel Wangchuck has the better of me. The son of Jigme Singye, the fifth king of Bhutan is apparently a *huge* fan of mountain biking, particularly the annual Tour of the Dragon race, where cycling maniacs rush from Bumthang in the east of the country to the capital, Thimphu. It's a 268-kilometre ride that – despite ludicrous ups and downs – is completed in a day. Biking is booming; it's Bhutan's big thing.

So what am I doing here? This is no place for a dilettante. These are the Himalayas I'm pedalling up and down, for goodness sake; it's like going from flying a kite to piloting an F-15 fighter plane with no training in between. In truth, I hadn't thought I'd make it to the top of any mountains – and certainly hadn't considered pursuing the activity to the point of danger. Instead, I'd come to Bhutan intent on writing a story about a country where many of those subsistence farmers live several hours' walk from a road; where prayer flags flutter over wire bridges and prayer wheels creak and spin; where rice terraces adorn the slopes and temples stand grey in the morning mist; and where deep valleys cleft a landscape that's puckered and folded and pressed and contorted and pushed up into the highest mountains in the world.

On the plane from Delhi, the pilot had pointed out Everest on our left. Even viewed at a distance, nose pressed against my tiny double-glazed plastic window, Everest looked pretty darn Everesty: square and stern, part of a seriously monumental bit of planet. At that moment I became convinced that my puny pedalling skills would be shown up immediately. Others more powerful of thigh would take the initiative while I rode in the back of the truck we'd been promised. I'd put pen to paper, while others put pedal to metal – or whatever the cycling equivalent was.

Yet here I am, hurtling down, down, down. I may not be wearing anything reflective, but you may be pleased to know that I am wearing a helmet. Not that I've encountered any traffic police, apart from a man directing matters at a crossroads in central Thimphu. Other than stuff about dragons, the guidebooks make a great play of the fact that this chap is the human equivalent of the only traffic light in the country. Red-amber-green means nothing here; the road signs are also somewhat haphazard, set at rakish angles.

A few days before, a man called Yarab had kitted us out with what were, to be honest, somewhat underwhelming hardtail bikes. Scuffed, battered – well let's just say the Australian was looking pretty smug as he polished his own bouncing beast. For his part, Yarab didn't seem too concerned about anything very much. 'The journey is the happiness,' he told me. 'Not the destination.' Well, for this journey I'd bought a pair of padded lycra shorts

– my first foray into cycling synthetics. Hot and rather chafing, they didn't make me feel happy at all.

However, my shorts and I loosened up a bit on our sedate tour of the terraced fields of the Paro Valley, where it's still a novelty to see Westerners making fools of themselves. Infants waved as if my sideburns reminded them of Bradley Wiggins; old men grinned, teeth stained red with betel nut juice; schoolchildren tittered in their neat, pressed uniforms. We paused regularly for cows to be herded past us, and also to admire a strange procession of bright red phalluses painted on walls for good luck.

The real event was still to come. It would take more than a comedy penis, I suspected, for me to navigate the climb from Thimphu to the Dochla Pass, along what was laughably called the National Highway – all of one-and-a-half lanes wide. I slept uneasily that night, disturbed by Bhutan's after-dark chorus of barking dogs.

In the end, though, Chris got me through it; he'd done bits of the route of the Tour de France in the past, he said, and was certainly frighteningly fit. He was soon talking me upwards; indeed, I quickly realised that all you need to cycle twenty-three kilometres up a mountain is a bit of company. And quite a lot of rest stops. And cereal bars. And water. Lots of water. The lycra shorts didn't help at all.

From swathes of blue pine and green oak, we progressed to thickets of rhododendron and then sparser vegetation as the air thinned. I won't deny it: it hurt quite a lot. Pain swelled along the backs of my thighs, in my arms and in my lungs. Yarab would occasionally circle back – he got to the top twice in the time it took me – to chide me onwards.

Now, though, lost in the night and plummeting back downwards from the summit, I'm genuinely worried that I've taken a wrong turning – not that I'd seen any options left or right. My wife would not be pleased at my situation. We've got kids, you know. Two of them: both young, both boys, both perfectly capable of doing stupid things on bicycles. I hold hands with them on the way to school, and we wait patiently for the Green Man before crossing the road. She might think I should be setting them an example, not hurling myself off a mountain out of misplaced bravado.

I wonder, suddenly, what the small print of my insurance policy says about cycling off the side of a 3,140-metre-high mountain in the dark. Is it under the same section as trampolining, or is it more like base jumping? Perhaps I can make amends for my foolishness by enrolling the boys on a cycling proficiency course the minute I get home – assuming I get home.

But you know what? If I'm honest, at this moment I am utterly, inexcusably, glad that it is dark. I am, in a delirious, irresponsible, almost unhinged way, relishing the extraordinary difference between this black-blanketed mountainside and home. Travel insurance, parental responsibility – both are, really, not what being in Bhutan is all about. It's as if, by being a third of the way around the world, a string has snapped between me and my life in London. In real jeopardy for once, I feel utterly alive. This, I tell myself, breathlessly as I hurtle on, is why I love to travel; this is why I came here. To exist in this moment.

I push on, speed up. Now, perhaps, I'm taking more risks on the corners. My heart pounds faster. It's the adrenalin talking, of course: the sum of two hours of exhausted pedalling upwards, then this foolish downward plunge; the reverse equivalent of the bends.

Normal service is often suspended when we travel; we sense danger differently. Yes, we'd be rightly scared walking down an unfamiliar street at night, but at the same time we can be strangely relaxed at not wearing a seat belt in a taxi in Dubai, or choosing to ride pillion on a moped in Vietnam, or deciding – unaccountably – to take up bungee jumping for an afternoon in New Zealand's Queenstown. Our inbuilt road signs become wonkier the further we are from home, a match for Bhutan's any day.

In this brief moment of clarity, I've just remembered the place where I am falling to. Punakha, one-time capital of Bhutan. I hope they serve beer.

Perhaps unsurprisingly, the beer in Bhutan is also called Druk. Once you're on a roll with a dragon theme, I guess it's hard to stop. If I live through this, I'll need to celebrate – and what better place to toast my continued existence than in a tiny town in the middle of nowhere?

'From Dochula to Punakha is fifty kilometres,' Yarab had said, gesturing forward as he welcomed me to the top of the mountain. Panting, my legs weak, my mouth dry, I'd looked up, following the line of his arm. Beyond a hundred or so squat grey chortens lay spread a snow-clad panorama of Himalayas far mightier than the hill I'd just managed. 'There,' said Yarab, gesturing to the row of sharp, white shark's teeth, 'is Kang Bum. And there,' he pointed, 'is Gangkhar Puensum, the highest in Bhutan.'

It's a vision – clear blues and whites, stark in their clarity – that will stay with me for a long time. Yes, yes, it made the slog to the summit worthwhile, but a good view will do that the world over. More pertinently, I have never felt so small. Close up or far away, the Himalayas always offer a humbling sense of perspective.

We were late to the viewpoint, though, the result of my low-geared, wheezing, upward journey. The Australian was long gone, helter-skelter down the other side, and Yarab was concerned that night was falling. 'When it gets dark, you should stop,' he said. 'The support truck can take us the rest of the way to Punakha.'

Words uttered long ago now. Night falls fast in the Himalayas, and the support truck and I are far, far apart. Out there in the dark, the highest mountain in Bhutan watches over us. Unseen in the velvety night, its bulk towers over me, over Chris, over the Australian and his headcam, over Yarab and the HGVs.

Prayer wheels spin and flags flutter in the night-time breeze. A country founded on belief systems utterly unlike my own prepares for slumber: breathes in, breathes out. I am a mote on its surface, a dark, buzzing insect: careless, flying further into the night. And I am, in my own way, enlightened.

The journey is the happiness, not the destination. I pedal downwards, towards the valley floor.

Ben Ross is Head of Print for Telegraph Travel (*The Daily Telegraph* and *The Sunday Telegraph*). He was previously Travel Editor of *The Independent* and *The Independent on Sunday*. He began writing about travel in 2001.

Bedtime Stories in Little Tibet
Dervla Murphy

*O*ne winter, Dervla Murphy and her six-year-old daughter Rachel, along
with the pony Hallam, explored 'Little Tibet' high up in the Karakoram
Mountains in the frozen heart of the Western Himalayas, on the Pakistan side
of the disputed border with Kashmir. Dervla chose to travel in winter to avoid
other tourists. For three months they travelled along the perilous Indus Gorge
and into nearby valleys, beset by sub-zero temperatures, ferocious winds and
whipping sands. Where the Indus is Young *was first published in 1977.*
Dervla writes:

> My relatives and friends made no comment but quite a few readers felt
> obliged to protest on Rachel's behalf. One likened her participation in the
> Balti trek to the use of child chimney sweeps. Another questioned my general
> 'fitness to mother'. A third hinted at some only half-suppressed inclination
> towards infanticide. A few thought UNICEF or Save the Children should
> look into the matter... Now, forty years later, several EU child protection
> laws would doubtless be quoted. Just a few months ago, Rachel astonished
> me by writing a very beautiful poem precisely recalling the physical setting
> of one of her more hazardous experiences. I'm happy to say her own three
> teenage daughters are not and never have been overprotected.

From Chapter 2 – Dropped in the Indus Gorge
Our Christmas dinner consisted of chapattis and a watery dahl gruel,

followed by watery tea. Seemingly they never rise to meat in Juglote, even for Id. But as this was our first meal in twelve hours it tasted remarkably good.

Then the proprietor led Rachel and me across a narrow yard to a room in which no progressive Irish farmer would keep pigs. The stone walls are smeared with dung and mud and for ventilation we have a tiny, high-up unglazed window and a 'chimney' hole in the roof. (There are signs on the sanded floor that some guests bring their own wood and make their own fires.) One corner is occupied by a tall pile of quilts, for hire to those without bedding, and we are sharing this suite with Mohammad at a cost of Rs3 for each sagging charpoy, which is expensive by local standards. To get to bed everyone has to clamber over everyone else's charpoy and two of my ropes collapsed as Mohammad was on his way across, just a few moments ago.

Earlier, as I was reading Rachel her bedtime story (a ritual which unfailingly takes place in the most unlikely surroundings), we heard through the gloom weird, unhuman movements and utterances close beside us in this supposedly empty room. Rachel went rigid with fright and even I was momentarily unnerved. Then I resolutely swung my torch towards the sound – and discerned a speckled hen settled for the night on that pile of quilts and engaged in a vigorous flea-hunt.

From Chapter 3 – **Alarms and Excursions**

Two hours later we were again on the edge of the Gorge, and now my heart sank at the prospect of negotiating that unspeakable path. Descents are always more difficult and Akbar had gone far ahead with a Mendi friend. Holding Rachel's right hand (the drop was on our left), I moved down slowly and steadily, trying to keep my eyes off the river – which was not easy, since its noise and movement had an hypnotic effect. All went well until we came to a point some 250 feet above the water where the path simply ceases to exist. For a distance of perhaps two yards – only two brave, carefree steps! – one has to negotiate a cliff-face on which a bird could hardly perch. The rock has been worn smooth by generations of brave, carefree Mendi feet and this bulge overhangs the river so prominently that it is impossible not to look down, and my giddiness was increased by the sight of all those lumps of icy snow swirling and whirling below us. To circumvent the bulge one has to arch one's body outwards, while keeping one's head lowered to avoid the overhang, and there is no handhold of any kind.

As I crouched there, with one foot on the slippery polished rock, trying to work out how to get by without releasing Rachel's hand, a terrible, nightmarish paralysis suddenly overcame me. I felt that I could neither go on, nor, because of Rachel, retreat up the path, which just behind us was only marginally less appalling. I realized that I had completely lost my nerve, for the first time ever, and it was an indescribably dreadful sensation – by far the most terrifying experience of a not unduly sheltered lifetime. The next stage (I was on the very verge of it) would have been pure panic and almost certain disaster. But then Rachel asked, altogether out of the blue as is her wont – 'Mummy, how are torpedoes made exactly?' And this question may well have saved our lives by momentarily taking my mind off the Indus.

I was afraid to turn my head, lest Rachel might be infected by the fear on my face. I simply gave my standard reply to such technological questions – 'I've absolutely no idea, darling' – and the sound of my own voice uttering those familiar words at once steadied me. As Akbar stared at us from the landing-stage I shouted, 'Please take Rachel!' and he raced up the cliff. I passed Rachel to him across that horrific stretch of non-path and the moment she was safe regained my nerve. Nonchalantly manoeuvring myself around the bulge, I cheerfully imagined that if I did fall in I could probably swim out. But I shall never forget those paralysed moments.

From Chapter 8 – **Skardu to Khapalu**

When we were at last admitted to our room seven men followed us, oozing friendly curiosity and taking up so much space that I had no room to

14

unpack. As Rachel was almost asleep on her feet I had to ask them to leave after ten minutes, though they were obviously longing to examine our belongings and see how and what we ate for supper. On this last score they were not missing anything. Rachel had already had her supper of dried apricots while we were waiting outside, and mine consisted of two dog-biscuits and a kettle of tea.

At noon we came to one of those intimidating stretches where the track has been built up on stakes driven into a rocky wall rising sheer out of the Shyok, which swirls rapidly past, hundreds of feet below. Here a jeep came over the highest point of the track, some twenty yards above us, without warning. (We had been unable to hear it over the roar of the river.) Hallam snorted with terror and reared up and I looked around to see him on his hind legs with Rachel poised over the water far below. Even to recall that vision now makes me feel sick. There has been no nastier moment in my entire forty-three years. As the jeep-driver jammed on the brakes Hallam recovered himself. Rachel dismounted and I beckoned the driver to help me unload, since a loaded animal could not pass the vehicle. Then I slowly led Hallam – still trembling and with ears laid back – along the edge of the precipice and over the top. There the track mercifully widened, allowing us to reload in safety. Meanwhile Rachel had dissolved into tears of fright and if ever an occasion called for loving maternal reassurance this was it. But I am deeply ashamed to relate that I rounded savagely on the poor child and told her to stop behaving like a baby. Human nature can be very unattractive.

From Chapter 11 – Kiris to Skardu

Skardu – 10 March

This morning saw an historic event of enormous interest: the removal by the Misses Murphy of their clothes, after almost three months. Rachel was disappointed – 'Our *bodies* don't look dirty! It's all on our vests!' Apparently one does not get progressively dirtier in a very cold climate. That protective coating of oil which establishes itself on the skin seems to repulse dirt. There was of course nothing to be done with our underclothes but drop them on the midden outside, from where they will soon be retrieved by some fuel-hunter. I decided against washing before putting on clean garments. Who knows what temperatures we may encounter up the Shigar Valley?

Today's weather has been vile. It snowed wetly and continuously, the low sky was almost black and the icy damp seemed to chill one's very marrow. Walking around the town was neat hell, with deep sticky mud trying to drag one's boots off, or skiddy mud making it impossible to keep upright even with a stick.

From Chapter 12 – Spring comes to the Shigar Valley

Yuno – 16 March

At times the language barrier gives an unreal tinge to events. While we stood under an enormous *chenar*, in the sudden grey coolness that comes when the sun has slipped behind the mountains, our 'guardian' conducted a vigorous and lengthy argument with several shrill-voiced women who glared at us from the edge of their roof as though we had the plague. Everybody spoke so quickly and vehemently that I could gather nothing of what was being said, but obviously we were extremely unwelcome. I was about to suggest to Rachel that we should push on to the next hamlet, visible three miles away, when our 'guardian' suddenly shook both his fists at the women and shouted some infuriated threat which abruptly ended the argument. He then beckoned us up the steep path to their house, which has a new room built on to the original structure and seems to be the poshest in the hamlet.

While I was unloading and unsaddling – none of the dozen men standing around offered to help – Rachel found that the new wing is entered through a window. The men whispered and sniggered while they watched me carrying the load and tack to the room, which is about ten feet by thirty and has a big over-fed woodstove. Soon Rachel and I were sweltering, so accustomed have we become to living in cold rooms and depending on our clothes for warmth. While writing this – on the floor, by the light of my own candle, in a corner as far as possible from the stove – I am dripping sweat; and poor Rachel, though exhausted, is unable to sleep because of the heat plus noise. Everyone in the family seems to have a wracking cough – inevitable, when they exchange this temperature for the Balti cold while clad only in rags.

To revert to our arrival. The first person I saw in the room was Blue Suit, sitting scowling on the edge of the charpoy beside the stove. Our reluctant host and hostess are his grandparents and his return to Yuno is provoking extraordinarily intense emotion; everyone who comes to greet him bursts into tears – men and women alike – as they press him to their bosoms and kiss him fondly.

As I was unpacking the stove to make tea Blue Suit asked brusquely, 'Are you Muslim?', and my reply generated a perceptible current of antagonism. Previously I have experienced this sort of bigotry only in Eastern Turkey; it is far less common than anti-Muslim writers would have us believe, though when it does occur it can make one feel wretchedly ill-at-ease. When I held out our kettle and politely requested *chu* everybody in the crowded room stared at me, without moving or speaking, for some moments. Then Blue Suit said, 'Here there is no water. Why do you not go to the next village? They have water. And there you can find Rest House. It is one mile only.' By this stage I was wishing that we had gone on, but having unpacked – and already paid an outrageous Rs10 for very inferior fodder – I had no intention of being hustled away. Besides I know the next hamlet does not have a Rest House and is at least three miles further up the valley.

Rachel's reaction to 'no *chu*' was robust – 'You can't have a village without water!' And picking up our *dechi* she climbed through the window and vanished. Fifteen minutes later she returned, looking puzzled, with the *dechi* packed full of off-white snow. 'It's true,' she said. 'There's no stream, no irrigation channel, no well. I had to go down to the fields for snow. But I dug below the surface so it won't be too dirty.' Daughters have their uses.

Sidi – 17 March

What a night that was! Rachel had collapsed into an uneasy sleep just before I squeezed down beside her on a mud floor carpeted only with thick dust. For the next three hours I lay in sweaty misery while the stove was kept red-hot and the hookah continued to bubble and the company continued to argue. Repeatedly I reached the edge of sleep only to be jerked back from it by heat and noise and fleas. At one stage the Kashmir problem was being passionately discussed and I gathered – because Blue Suit was giving all the latest Pindi news – that today there is to be a general *hartal* of Muslims in India, organized by Mr Bhutto.

It was 1.40 a.m. before everyone (except our host) had settled down on the floor. We were nineteen, not counting the numerous babies who had contributed their share to the evening's din and continued to give tongue at intervals throughout what remained of the night. I was enduring an agony of thirst, for which there was no remedy, and when I at last fell into a doze I was awakened by a powerful kick on the nose from Rachel. This caused such a spectacular haemorrhage that I had to remove my socks to mop up. It really was quite a night; definitely among my Top Ten for sheer discomfort.

When the men had gone on their way we remained by the water, stoically masticating apricots while Hallam enjoyed his oats. He is now much the best-fed member of the expedition; lifting Rachel into the saddle, I notice that she weighs about half what she did three months ago.

The sun was hot and the air sparkling as we continued down the valley. Despite our 'defeat', I count this among the best of many wonderful Balti days; and it emphasized the curious fact that here neither hunger nor lack of sleep seem to matter. Is this owing to the altitude or to the euphoria engendered by Baltistan's beauty? Whatever the cause, it is most convenient to live on a plain so exalted that after an hour's sleep one can effortlessly walk twenty-two miles on three fistfuls of apricots.

Shigar – 18 March

It was another restless night. I lay squeezed between Rachel and the three-year-old, whose frequent wretched whimperings in my ear were augmented by his sister's no less frequent spasms of coughing and crying. During the small hours our host summoned his wife, but when no longer needed she returned to the floor. All the time I was being tormented by fleas who have come out of hibernation with appetites like lions, and Rachel tossed and muttered and scratched in her sleep though she never actually woke.

Shigar – 19 March

Among the glories of this Rest House is a roll of pale pink loo-paper, left here last summer by one of the tourists (an American girl and a Frenchman) entered in the Register for 1974. Rachel asked excitedly, 'How did *this* get here?', and when I explained she curled her lip. 'They must've been cissies to put *loo-paper* in their luggage!'

'It doesn't follow,' I said mildly. 'Not everyone has been brought up the hard way, on snowballs and stones.'

Life in Baltistan certainly teaches one to adapt a few possessions to many uses: I can think of no better antidote to the West's gadget-demented subculture. Our sack, for instance, is officially a sack – if you follow me – but in its off-duty hours it becomes, according to prevailing conditions, a window-curtain, a tablecloth, a mattress, a pillow, a horse-blanket or a floor-covering to protect new Rest House carpets from my culinary activities. Similarly, the lid of the old Complan tin used as a tea-caddy also serves as a mirror (the inside) and a candle holder (the outside), while our frying-pan serves as Hallam's grain-dish, and our kettle as tea-pot, and our nailbrush as clothes-brush, saucepan-cleaner, boot-brush and potato scrubber, and our *dechi* as wash-up basin and, *in extremis*, as chamber-pot. Possibly the time is nearer than we think for the Western world to learn how expendable are most of its newfangled gadgets.

Skardu – 21 March

For us Now Ruz ended on a sordid note, Rachel was abed and I had just begun this entry when a pathetic small voice said, 'What's biting me doesn't feel like fleas.' I took up my candle to examine the victim and the bites did not *look* like fleas, either. So I lit another candle, the better to hunt and found Rachel's clothes literally *crawling* with tiny grey body-lice. This was an extremely serious situation. I threw away all those filthy garments we removed before going to Shigar, so at present we have only the clothes we stand up (and lie down) in. Having made sure that the victim's skin was lice-free, I thrust her, naked and shivering, into my flea-bag. Then I stripped to examine my own garments. Mercifully these are not lice-infested, though I caught three fleas, and Rachel is now comfortably asleep in my vest and sweater under her own snow-suit. Body-lice are well named; there was not one louse on her pants, tights and stockings, despite the swarming mass of grey horrors on her upper garments. I dropped the infested clothes in a far corner of the field; first thing tomorrow they must be boiled. I find I react quite differently to fleas and lice. There is something so irresistibly comical about fleas that one can feel no real animosity towards them; a flea-hunt is a form of sport, demanding considerable skill, and one has to admire the creatures' cheeky agility. But those slow grey crawlers this evening really revolted me.

Reprinted from Where the Indus is Young *by Dervla Murphy, by kind permission of Eland Publishing Limited, 61 Exmouth Market, London EC1R 4QL. © Dervla Murphy 1977*

Dervla Murphy was born in 1931 in Ireland, and was educated at the Ursuline Convent in Waterford until she was fourteen, when she left to keep house for her father and to nurse her mother, who suffered from arthritis. On her mother's death in 1963 she cycled to India where she worked with

Tibetan refugee children. Her first book, *Full Tilt: Ireland to India with a Bicycle*, was published in 1965. Over twenty other titles have followed and she has won worldwide praise for her writing. Now in her eighties and still living in County Waterford, she continues to travel the world and remains passionate about politics, conservation, bicycling and beer. Her daughter, Rachel, and three granddaughters join Dervla on her travels when possible.

Negotiating on a Knife-Edge
Paul Davies

We'd been warned: everyone gets mugged in Rio. Everyone. It's simply part of the experience, like seeing the sunset over Sugarloaf or posing like a prize fool in front of the statue of Christ. Not that this warning had the slightest effect as we rolled round a corner into darkness... and into trouble.

This is Lapa. The pulsating, partying heart of Brazil's sexiest city. All along the cobbled, bar-fringed streets, thumping basslines battle each other for territory as a mob of beer hawkers marches up and down to the beat, honing in on gap-year students only too happy to trade their savings for a stream of envy-inducing Facebook updates.

On my left sits Henry, a merry mix of every student who's ever swapped life in Fulham for a life On The Road, confidently quaffing cocktails and using seasons as verbs. Next to Henry is German Martin, a man Evelyn Waugh would have described as appallingly sane and for whom discussion of the exchange rate unfortunately got mistaken for an acceptable icebreaker. The rest of the night's round table comprises shoestring-adventurers Alice the Canadian and a brace of Danish dames whose names I originally took to be an exotic drinks order and subsequently forgot entirely.

Ignited by caipirinhas, conversation is a blazing bonfire of blissfully illogical inanities. Time gets lost in Lapa like few other places I've known, blown along by the wild and sweaty spirits that romp through the humid streets. Within a few hours, our descent into a debauched haze of recklessness and irresponsibility is complete – even my most English of feet are affected, amateurishly dancing around like the jumbled letters on the page of a teenage poet.

I don't know when to stop, and Lapa certainly never has and presumably never will. Martin and the – by now irretrievably intoxicated – females nevertheless do and order a retreat. The sensible call in this situation is undoubtedly to head for the taxi rank. However, shoestrings and sense can be confusing companions and the bus stop beckons. As does a worrisome wait, when what eventually heads towards us is not a bus, but an advancing mob of youthful Brazilian bravado. Armed, dangerous and, in Henry's understated words, 'distinctly unwelcome'.

The fury in the gang's steps and the violence in their eyes tell us that this is not a good time to be joking around. As their shadows encroach on our swaying circle, my guts spin in harmony with the inside of my head – and that's before I see the knife. The tip is first a barely perceptible flash of light reflecting the wan streetlamp, before being suddenly brandished into the open and into my face.

'*Prata. Prata.*' Silver. Silver.

That's the beauty of the Brazilian street child – no airs and graces, no complicated set-up, just straight to business. Knives can cut through opening social salvos just as sharply as they slice open the organs of those audacious enough to try to protect their pockets.

As the only Portuguese speaker around, it's up to me to do something about this. I stall (and panic). Luckily, stalling comes more easily to a tongue tied up with fear and with additional shaking and slurring added in for good measure.

'*Não entendo. Quer um prato?*' You want a plate?

Amid a stuttering exchange of Portuguese pleasantries, it becomes encouragingly clear: these kids are still new to the game – as much tourists in their own gangster lifestyle as we are in this sleazy side street of their city. The boy's grip on the knife loosens and with it the gang's grip on the situation. It's a momentary reprieve. Hanging around an unpredictable boy with a blade on a shadowy South American street is still scary enough to inspire prayer in even the most ardent atheist. When the scene is eventually lit up by the heavenly headlights of the otherwise rudimentary bus, I begin to understand why the whole country is Catholic.

Urgently bustling into the ramshackle tin shed on wheels, we veer off into an impromptu rally through Rio, whisked away by a man with the look of someone who wished he'd paid more attention in school, just as we wished we'd paid more attention to the warnings... and wondered whether we'd truly dodged the danger after all.

After an English upbringing that rarely took him farther afield than family holidays in Wales, or Cambridge during his university years, Paul has spent the last decade escaping the grey skies of London whenever possible. He recently moved to Qatar to work, to  explore the Middle East and to experience a life without bacon. He is still to find a cure for his addiction to South America. His story found its way into this collection after being entered into a Bradt/ *Independent on Sunday* Travel Writing Competition.

The Locked Trunk
in the Forest

Adrian Phillips

It was 11.30 a.m. on a summer's day in Canada when I discovered that the only way to open the boot of a Chrysler Sebring hard-topped convertible is by pressing a button on its black key fob. I discovered this a moment after closing the boot with the black key fob inside. I could picture the fob sitting neatly on top of my suitcase. Nevertheless, I patted my pockets in the hope it had somehow spawned a twin. I ran my fingers around the boot in search of a hidden handle. I retraced my steps across the car park, scanning the ground for the thing I knew was somewhere else. And then I put my hands to my head in a state of welling panic and fought the urge to have a good cry.

People tend to assume a travel writer spends his life sprawled in beachside hammocks killing time between cocktails and seafood suppers. But behind the juicy bits in the magazine spreads are a thousand cuttings on the floor of the writer's memory: cramped flights, upset stomachs, toadying emails to editors, tedious meetings with hotel managers, missed buses, drop toilets, lost passports, colourless museums, aching feet, endless scrawls in countless notebooks. Keys locked in hire cars parked in the middle of unfamiliar places. Pressing deadlines.

Eleven forty and the clock was ticking. I'd been commissioned to write a feature about a tree-top canopy walk deep in the Highlands of Ontario, and so early that morning I had collected a hire car and set out from Toronto.

It was a four-hour drive, the city's glass and concrete spinning free, replaced by a thickening wilderness of pine trees that I knew hid big black bears and packs of wolves on the prowl. My guide and his group would be leaving the visitor centre of the Haliburton Forest Reserve at 1 p.m. sharp – the sharpness had been stressed to me – but, with time in hand, I stopped at a solitary store to buy some wine for the evening. That's when it happened. I popped the boot of the locked car, laid down the fob while I wedged the bottles between my bags – and slammed the boot shut. I was eight miles short of my destination.

Standing by the car, I tried to ignore the butterflies buffeting the inside of my stomach and assess the options before me. Option One: complete the remaining eight miles on foot. This was an unappealing prospect, certainly, but it wouldn't be impossible to cover the ground in time if I jogged parts of the way. However, by the time I returned night would have fallen, the store would have closed and I'd have no-one for company but big black bears and packs of wolves on the prowl. I crossed Option One off the list. Option Two: reschedule the canopy walk. Out of the question, unfortunately, because I had no contact number for the guide and I was anyway flying home the following day. Option Three: find a light-fingered boot cracker who could retrieve the key – and quickly.

A cashier from the store phoned Henry, who arrived at midday in a black pick-up truck with a hook hanging from a little crane at the back. He was a reassuring figure, with a brimming box of tools, oil-smeared dungarees and an expression I interpreted as one of heroic altruism. 'It's great to see you! I've locked my key in the trunk,' I explained, adopting the local lingo. Henry didn't answer. Instead he walked around the car, peering through each of the windows, before returning to my side.

'How do you plan to pay?' he said, avoiding any opening niceties. On reflection, I decided there was something weaselly about Henry's expression.

'You don't take cards, I suppose?'

'Nope.'

'I'm afraid I've only twenty dollars in cash. Will that cover it?' Henry just shrugged, and then got to work.

His first act was to test each of the door handles, working on the theory that this wouldn't have occurred to an imbecile from England with only twenty dollars in his wallet. To Henry's surprise, the doors remained unmoved. Next he pulled from his bag a flat piece of metal that he attempted to slide into the door mechanism from the bottom of the driver's window. But the gap was too narrow. Finally he turned to a long piece of thick wire, forcing one end between the top of the window and its seal, and feeding it down towards the unlock button on the inside of the door panel.

Henry crouched with forehead pressed to the glass and tongue sticking through white whiskers as he attempted to prod the button with the skinny finger of metal. It was a painstaking, teeth-grinding process. Several times the wire landed on its target only to slide away, a string of muttered swear words trailing in its wake. But after twenty minutes of near misses there was a satisfying clunk. With a smug glance in my direction, Henry lifted the door handle, and triggered a cacophony that sent him leaping like a hairy salmon.

The blaring rhythm of a car alarm commands urgency. A flustered Henry hurried into the driver's seat and jabbed at the 'open trunk' button on the steering column. Nothing happened. He pushed it again and again, but the electrics evidently only worked with the key in the ignition. He clambered awkwardly into the back, hunting for a lever to drop the seats and gain access to the boot. But this was a convertible and the roof-raising gear sat behind the rear seats, so they didn't lower. The alarm continued its loud complaint, supported by angry orange blinks from the hazard lights; a sprinkle of shoppers gathered to watch.

'You'll have to phone the rental company,' Henry said above the din as he emerged defeated and red-cheeked from the car. He was right, I knew; we'd exhausted all other options. I punched the digits into my mobile, but the line wouldn't connect.

'I think it's because I'm using a foreign mobile,' I explained to Henry. His non-foreign mobile sat on the bonnet of his truck while he rolled a cigarette. He looked at it, and then at me.

'There's a phone booth about 200 metres up the road there,' he nodded. I felt the prickle of frustrated tears somewhere behind my eyeballs.

'But I've no change, Henry.'

He carefully licked the length of his cigarette paper, before reaching into the front of his dungarees. 'Here's a quarter,' he said, and turned away to find a lighter.

Those were a lonely 200 metres, trudged listlessly in the knowledge the game was up. The clock and Chrysler and Henry and the world were against me. It was 12.30; there was no way the car rental company could send help in time for me to make the canopy walk. The sun had disappeared behind a bank of gloomy cloud and the branches of the pine trees drooped like sagging shoulders. Why had I stopped for booze? What would I file to the editor? I'd have no tale to tell of a hike through the treetops, nothing to show for the cost of my flight. Of course, in the greater scheme of things this was no disaster; I hadn't been kidnapped by pirates or bitten by a rabid racoon. But life isn't always lived with an eye on its greater scheme, and at that helpless moment in that strange place there seemed no worse a predicament.

'Good afternoon, how are you doing today?' chirruped an irritatingly upbeat voice on the other end of the line.

'I've locked my key in the boot.'

'The boot?'

'The trunk.'

'Oh, poor you! Have you tried pushing the "open trunk" button?'

Patience; he's only trying to help. 'Yes.'

'And pulling the seats down?'

'Yes.'

'Hmmm, in which case I'm all outta ideas!' he declared with a cheery laugh, before putting me on hold while he contacted the Chrysler manufacturers. I stared into space with the phone to my ear, listening to Shania Twain sing about various things that men do that don't impress her much.

A sharp knock on the booth made me jump. 'Hey, I've got your key out!' said an excited man outside. I recognised him as one of the shoppers; he'd managed to shine a flashlight into the trunk through a small space between the back seats, he panted as we hurried back to the store, and hooked the fob with Henry's wire. There were still twenty minutes to get to the visitor centre and the game was back on; I could have kissed his round, pink face.

Henry was waiting at the car with the key. 'That'll be forty dollars for my time,' he said, and my smile drained into the gutter.

'But I've only got twenty dollars. You know that.'

He shrugged his trademark shrug, a cigarette in one hand – and my key tucked snug in the other. The butterflies made a fresh assault upon my stomach lining. I cast a desperate eye on the ground, seeking inspiration or a twenty-dollar bill, and then dashed into the store.

'Do you do cashback?'

'Cashback, sir?' said the owner blankly, rolling the words in his mouth like a cow chewing cud.

'Yes! Can you charge an amount on a card and give that in cash?'

The bovine owner pondered, rubbing a hand down his long face. 'Yes, sir, we can do that.'

'Wonderful!' I handed him my debit card. He stared at it for a while, the cogs of his mind turning slowly as the precious seconds passed; I imagined his tail swishing lazily at flies behind the counter. 'But not on debit cards.'

It was the only card I had. 'OK, OK. What if I buy something and overpay – could you give me the difference in cash?' Again the cogs made their labouring circuit as Mr Moo considered things. 'Yes, sir, we can do that.'

'Excellent!'

'But not on debit cards.'

If I'd had a towel, I'd have thrown it in. The group would be heading out in fifteen minutes, eyes peeled for wolf and bear, and I was stuck here facing a cow-like man who... 'Of course, we've got an ATM,' Mr Moo volunteered as a long-delayed afterthought. 'Would that help?'

The ATM stood in the corner of the store. *Enter your code.* Done, quick as a flash. *Select amount.* Done. *Do you accept the charge for using this private ATM?* Yes. Yes, yes, just hurry up! *Transaction processing – please wait...* An interminable delay, much shuffling and whirring in the belly of the machine, the clicking return of the card. *Transaction denied.* I tried again; maybe the machine would change its mind. *Enter your code. Select amount. Transaction processing – please wait... Transaction denied.* I had started a third time because, frankly, I had no other hands to play when a familiar voice spoke nearby.

'Look, I can lend you the money.' It was my pink-faced saviour from earlier, with a basket of beer in his hand and – although it might have been a trick of the light – a halo over his head.

'That's so kind, but I couldn't accept,' I stuttered.

'Sure you could. It's only twenty dollars.'

'No, I really couldn't.'

He shrugged – not a Henry shrug, but the sort of reluctant shrug hitched to a concerned look that the Good Samaritan might have given if the traveller lying beaten in the gutter had said, 'Don't worry, mate, I'll be fine down here.'

I watched in agony as he put his beer on the counter. *Should I change my mind?* He opened his wallet and passed a bill across to the cashier. *Last chance; soon he'd be gone forever.* The cashier opened the till to pass his change. And then it hit me.

'Stop! Excuse me!' I called, slipping over in my eagerness to cover the ground. They both hesitated, hands hanging in the air. I picked myself up and took a deep breath: 'What if I pay for your beer on my card and then you give me the money in cash?' There was a pause, a few long seconds of silence in which the idea settled and I waited for the inevitable flaws to float to its surface. But they never came. The man just broke into a broad grin, flashing teeth as white as the angel wings I knew must be concealed beneath his flannel lumberjack shirt.

'Yep, that would work perfect, and if you follow my car I'll get you to the visitor centre in time too.'

And he did – in fact, I arrived with a whole minute to spare. The magazine article was published a couple of months later, a piece describing the tranquillity to be found in the Highlands of Ontario. There was no mention of the less-than-tranquil preceding two hours; they were to remain cuttings on the floor of a travel writer's memory. But for all the splendour of Canada's towering trees and heavy-headed moose, it's the faces of those untold hours I'll remember best: those of Mr Moo, the kind stranger and the weasel Henry – whose quarter I never did return.

Adrian Phillips is Managing Director of Bradt Travel Guides, as well as an award-winning freelance writer and broadcaster whose articles have ranged from swamp-walking in the Everglades and forest trekking in Samoa to cork-harvesting in Portugal and going on seafood safari in Sweden. He contributes to many national newspapers and magazines, has a regular travel slot on BBC Radio 5 Live, and was voted Travel Writer of the Year in 2012.

The Letter Z

Catriona Rainsford

I was washing up in Elvira's courtyard when I heard the first shots. My curiosity had already been piqued by a hubbub of shouting and barking dogs in the street outside, but it was the shots that froze me, plate and sponge in hand, straining to catch some meaning in the confused and increasingly frantic noise. A couple of screams cut through the shouting. Slamming doors. Then more shots.

Trico crashed through the door from the kitchen, his friends Oscar and Chino close behind him. I had been living in his family home for much of the last few months. On that day we had just finished lunch, and they had been preparing drinks while I washed the pans and crockery. Trico's mother Elvira was visiting one of her sisters; his truck-driver father was away on a journey.

'Get inside, Cat,' Trico barked.

'What the –'

'Get *inside*.'

He pushed me, almost roughly, through the open door to the bedroom, then blocked the exit with his body as he stood in the doorway, peering towards the rooftop. The house was situated in a typical Mexican *barrio* (neighbourhood): a warren of flat-roofed houses and hidden courtyards, and each yard had a flight of external steps by which the residents could access the roof. Here, they would come to hang their washing, dispose of odd pieces of scrap, or get away from the extended family which circulated constantly through their homes. By way of the roof, one had access to at least twenty different yards and thirty different houses.

Oscar and Chino appeared behind me.

'It's on the street, isn't it?' Oscar asked.

The shouting on the street continued but there were now also closer noises, seeming to come from above, from the rooftop. Trico stood rigid, like an animal sniffing the air.

'I'm going to see.'

He crept up the concrete steps, stopping halfway to crane his neck, trying to see on to the level of the rooftop. Then he climbed a few steps further, almost to the top. Oscar pushed past me and went up to join him. I made as if to follow, but Chino held me back.

'Careful. Wait until we know what's going on.'

The shouts were fewer now, less confused but more urgent, sharp voices from the rooftop as well as more muffled ones from the street. Thuds. Another few shots. Trico and Oscar jumped down and came hurriedly back inside.

'What the fuck are they doing?' Trico exclaimed.

'What?'

'They're on the roof, throwing stones, bricks… they're firing at them from the street… what the *fuck* –'

'Who's firing?'

After several months in northern Mexico, I knew all too well the implications of gunfire. The violence between warring cartels had been escalating steadily since the time of my arrival, creeping ever outwards from its original epicentre on the trafficking route between the drug-growing regions of the Sierra Madre and the war-torn cities on the US border. Gunfire in Ciudad Juárez or Chihuahua had long been commonplace. But up until now, Trico's hometown of San Luis Potosí had remained a relatively peaceful backwater.

'Firing at who?' I persisted.

Before Trico could answer the tone of the noise changed again, the shouts welling into a panicked crescendo and then fading out, replaced by scuffling, running feet. Suddenly two young men I recognised from the area lurched into view, almost throwing themselves down the steps into the courtyard.

'Trico, man, they're coming on to the roof, you have to help us –'

'What the *fuck* –'

The residents of the barrio had all known each other since childhood, and their loyalty was unfailing. Even as he swore at them through clenched teeth, Trico was already pulling them inside and clicking the door closed behind them. He dropped to his knees and I followed, spurred by his urgency to copy him without asking questions. Together, we pulled out the bags and other bits and pieces we stored under the bed. The two men wriggled underneath, the last foot barely out of sight before we were frantically shoving the bags back in place to hide them from view. Then Trico hurried me into the living room along with Oscar and Chino. The four of us sat rigidly on the sofas. Doors closed. Television on.

Time is fickle in moments like this. How long did we sit there? Was it half an hour? An hour? Two hours? I couldn't say. There was a clock on the wall, but no-one was watching it. Nor did we watch the television. We looked at each other. The walls. The floor. It barely mattered, as our eyes were sightless. All of our energy was focused on listening, straining to pick up any clue from outside. My chest felt frozen and my head throbbed. The slightest rattle would give me a surge of nausea, in case it proved to be the precursor to the sequence of sounds I dreaded more than all others: the opening of the gate on to the road, purposeful footsteps across the entrance passage, and then a furious banging on the iron front door.

However long that lapse of time was, I felt as if it had aged me several years.

Eventually, Trico got slowly to his feet and walked softly over to the living room window. He tweaked the very edge of the net curtain and stood there in silence for several minutes. Then he crossed the room, cautiously opened the door to the courtyard and slipped outside. I assumed he must have crept up the steps to check the rooftop. I sat, rooted to the sofa. Even with the door open, it was deathly quiet outside. I pictured the whole neighbourhood, tense and listening just as we were.

I didn't stand up until I heard Trico pulling bags out from under the bed. I went through into the bedroom just as the two men were crawling out. Trico glared at them coldly.

'I think they've gone,' he said in a low voice. 'They're not on the rooftop anymore. But I wouldn't go on to the street for a while, just in case. What the fuck did you think you were doing?'

The two men, too tawny-skinned to go pale, were nevertheless looking distinctly grey.

'They must have been Zetas, man.'

The Zetas were a relatively new presence on the cartel scene, but had already gained a fearsome reputation. Originally comprised of defectors from the GAFE, an elite squad of Mexican paramilitaries trained and armed as part of counter-narcotics operations, they had been working as enforcers for the Gulf Cartel for the past ten years. After declaring their independence from the Gulf Cartel in February 2010, they had unleashed a wave of unprecedented brutality across eastern Mexico, starting in their home state of Tamaulipas and spreading south. Residents of San Luis had been discussing the development in increasingly low voices over the previous few weeks. All reached the same conclusion: it could only be a matter of time until the wave hit.

'Of course they were fucking Zetas,' Trico hissed. 'And you go throwing fucking bricks at them and then expect me to hide you. What do you think they would have done to us if they'd found you? What do you think they would have done to Cat?'

I had never seen him so enraged. I had seen him angry, of course – frequently with me. But usually it was a hot-blooded, hysterical anger that seemed almost pantomime in its melodrama and could be laughed about in retrospect. Now I saw icy fury. The men looked cowed. They had nothing to say.

'Get out.'

They didn't need telling twice. They fled up the steps to the roof, pausing at the top to check the coast was clear before running across it and disappearing from sight, crouched over as if in a warzone.

It was another hour before we felt safe to talk in normal voices, and several hours before we dared go on to the street. It turned out that the latter fear was not wholly unfounded. The only person who was 'taken' in the whole incident was a boy in his late teens who had been naive enough to go out to see what all the noise was about. He returned a short while later, badly beaten but at least alive. The overwhelming emotion on the street was one of relief. It could have been a lot worse.

I still don't really know what happened that day. No-one seemed to know, except possibly the men we had hidden, and they were keeping quiet. The men firing had been dressed as police. Were they police? Were they Zetas masquerading as police? Were they police infiltrated by Zetas, or acting on their commands? All of these scenarios were completely plausible.

From that day on, the cartel wars lost the soothing fog of abstraction that had previously surrounded them in my mind. I had been appalled by the stories, of course. But they had maintained the unreality of things happening to someone else, somewhere else. They had aroused many emotions in me – shock, anger, sadness, pity – but never the wrenching terror that throws you face to face with your own mortality and turns abstract horror into something sickeningly, viscerally real. It wasn't until that day that I truly understood what it felt like to think 'it could have been me'. And it was that thought that led inexorably to the still more chilling realisation: it could be anyone. Not, as the government would have had people believe, only those foolish enough (or, in the case of some journalists and honourable members of the authorities, brave enough) to get directly involved, but ordinary people living ordinary lives in ordinary streets. The rooftop where bricks had been thrown and shots fired was the same rooftop where Elvira hung her washing. The bed under which two men had cowered in fear for their lives was the same bed where I hugged Trico before going to sleep at night. The living room where we had sat for what seemed like eternity, rigid with fear as we waited for the bang on the door we felt sure was coming, was the same living room where Trico's two-year-old niece Jacky watched *Dora La Exploradora* on afternoon television.

It wasn't far away any more.

Catriona Rainsford was born in Cambridge. A promise made in a pub at closing time took her to Mexico, where a chance meeting began her two-year journey with street circus performers, the inspiration for her book *The Urban Circus: Travels with Mexico's Malabaristas* (of which the above is an extract), published by Bradt in 2013. She has won prizes for her travel writing in the Bradt/*Independent on Sunday* Travel Writing Competition in 2010 and *The Guardian* Travel Writing Competition in 2009.

Camel Mustering
in the Outback
Michael Palin

Iwake to the sound of galah birds (pink-throated, white-winged members of the parrot family) calling to each other like doors on squeaky hinges.

Over a swagman's breakfast – eggs, bacon and sausage cooked on a wood fire – Ian, dressed for the day in blue and white check shirt, jeans and trusty bush hat, promises me that what I am about to take part in is one of the greatest adrenalin rushes I shall ever experience. Westy doesn't help by adding that bungee jumping is tame compared to what we're going to do. It's the 'we' that alarms me. I can feel my sausages resurfacing as they speak.

At half past seven our armada of vehicles leaves camp and drives off down bumpy red earth tracks into the bush. This is Mad Max time. Wursty, wearing a turquoise cut-off and a scarf tied, bandana-style, beneath his baseball hat, drives a high chassis all-terrain Land Cruiser. Westy rolls up and down the column on a Yamaha 350, a black tube leading from his helmet to a water bag slung on his back. A helicopter is somewhere ahead of us, in the high wide skies, searching out the camels. Thin cassia trees provide the only escape from a hard unblinking sun. This is the sort of place where flying saucers land and things fall out of the sky. Land that is old and tired and has seen everything.

It's also Monty Python time. Even in my state of heightened anxiety I cannot hold back a smile as Ian strides to the top of a scrubby ridge, spreads his hand Moses-like out over the wilderness and declares: 'Great camel spotting country!'

There is a flurry of radio exchanges with the helicopter. Craig, the helicopter pilot, has spotted camel and they're heading in our direction. Ian beckons me towards his vehicle – a dusty, hard-worked, short-wheel base Toyota pick-up, known in this land of abbreviations as a 'shortie'. Attached to the screen is a fiercely explicit window sticker: 'Get In, Sit Down, Shut Up and Hang On'.

Immediately behind the cab are two parallel sets of metal bars and he orders me to stand between these alongside Gunnar. I'm handed a wooden stick about four feet long with a rope loop on the end which (and now there is no question of a choice in the matter) I must drop over the camel's head when Ian gets the vehicle close enough. In theory it sounds no more hazardous than a three-point turn but Ian's last words before he starts up give me a flavour of what's to come. 'When it's over his head for Christ's sake get down. If you get your body entangled with the rope it could take your leg off.'

Then we're off. Off the track, for a start. Ian blasts the shortie through the bush, cannoning up and down slopes, twisting and turning in pursuit of a bull camel which runs, rather than races, away from us with its nose in the air. Ian tries to match it movement for movement and, after a few desperate attempts, over which Ian screams advice, I make one last lunge which the camel disdainfully avoids. Westy and Wursty succeed where I have failed.

But Ian, I know, is not going to let me rest until I have lassoed my very own camel. We drive a little way further on before the next sighting. I cannot capture the sensation of what happens next better than in the lines I scribble in my notebook immediately afterwards.

Ian will simply not let me give up. Trying to keep my balance and rehang my stick lasso after the last attempt, I'm thrown one way and the other, banging the small of my back on the rear bar and the bottom of my ribcage on the front bar. Grabbing for a handhold only to be sent spinning by one of Ian's swerving high-speed ninety degree turns. Winded by the blow. Gasping for air as Ian yells at me to get ready. Pull myself upright, catch my balance, seize the forward bar just in time as he swings the wheel and accelerates so fast over a low rise that both my feet leave the floor. For one moment I want nothing more than to continue the ascent and rest quietly in the arms of St Peter.

Down to earth. Just in time to duck as we race under a low tree. Ian is almost up with three sprinting camels. He veers with them, I'm thrown forward, my rope loop hangs down over the cab, Ian shrieks at me to get it out of the way, before it catches in the steering wheel. Turns for another attempt. The camel's far too canny by now. Every pass is an effort. But no let up. After each failed pass he turns and takes me in again. I'm full of so much anger and frustration. Nowhere for it to go. Again Ian yells over the roar of the engine and the whine of the helicopter. 'Ready!'

The camels veer off as I throw. The vehicle spins and whines, flinging up the dust. I've hit my lower ribs going forward. The stick feels as heavy and unwieldy as a small tree. I want just to stop. Please let me stop. Ian readjusts his course and we fire onwards again. I'm pitched forward. He screams at me: 'Get that bloody rope out of the cab. I can't drive with it like that!' And that's when I explode. That's when all the pain and the anger and the emotion and frustration all comes out. I hurl abuse at Ian. I shriek Fs and Bs at him. I call him every foul name under the sun. But he probably can't hear for the screech of the tyres, the thumping of the helicopter, the whine of Westy's motor bike and the hysterical revving of the Land Cruiser. It's all pain and noise and desperation but now he has me alongside again, beautifully positioned. One last lunge, one last call on resources I don't believe I have and the loop is over! And then I know what he meant about adrenalin rushes. I know that everything is as he said it would be. I get down and clasp his shoulder and apologise for all I said, but he just beams and rubs the back of the lassoed camel and hands me a ball of fur. 'There y'are. Last of the winter coat.'

On our way to Alice Springs it's sunset and the rocks we pass glow like live coals. Though I know I shall be black and blue tomorrow I'm still buzzing with the exhilaration of what has been the most physically demanding day's filming in my life. What happened today was a rare experience, well outside the world we are all increasingly used to living in, a world of rules and regulations and sensible precautions. I was protected only by my own instinct and my trust in a group of people I barely knew.

I understand a little better now why people come out to earn a living in the burning heat of this hard, unfriendly land, why Ian and Westy and Wursty and the others still pit themselves physically against the camels instead of using, say, tranquillizing darts. There are easier ways to do it. But that's not the point.

Reprinted from Full Circle *by Michael Palin, by kind permission of The Orion Publishing Group, London. © Michael Palin, 1997*

Michael Palin established his reputation with *Monty Python's Flying Circus* and *Ripping Yarns*. His film work includes an award-winning performance as the hapless Ken in *A Fish Called Wanda* and, more recently, *American Friends* and *Fierce Creatures*. His television credits include two films for the BBC's *Great Railway Journeys*. He has written books to accompany his six very successful travel series, *Around the World in 80 Days, Pole to Pole, Full Circle, Hemingway Adventure, Sahara* and *Himalaya*. He is also the author of a number of children's stories, the play *The Weekend* and the novel *Hemingway's Chair*. www.palinstravels.co.uk

No Return from Nigeria

E T Laing

'**B**y the way,' he said, 'your ticket for Nigeria is only one way.'

He hesitated, seeming to watch for my reaction.

'But don't worry. Our staff in Lagos will look after you. They'll take you up over the border into Niger when you've finished. And then we'll get you a ticket out of Niger. We'll send it on to you later. It'll save us on airfares.'

I stared at him. Everyone had told me I was out of my mind to go there on my own. And now on a one-way ticket? But this was a *big* Lebanese construction company and the man in front of me was the manager of its smart London office: he must surely have known what he was doing. That was as far as my thoughts had taken me as he continued.

'Unless, of course, you feel... unhappy about it.' There was just a hint of a suggestion that I might be someone who needed his hand held.

'No,' I heard myself say. 'It'll be OK.'

But it wasn't, I thought, as I watched three exotically dressed women with massive hips brawling in the arrivals hall at Lagos airport. They were labouring to heave about ten huge boxes tied with rough twine off the carousel and screaming at each other for no apparent reason. Their menfolk stood to one side, intent on something more important. There were no white faces around me, and the eyes in the crowd seemed to look through mine. While other African airports are theatres of noisy, demonstrative reunions, here there was only apprehension, and bursts of ill-tempered banter. And my promised taxi was not to be seen. So in the end I had to make my own way in, to a shabby hotel with an air conditioner that clattered all night vomiting warm humid air and a shower that dribbled tepid brown water.

The next morning when I reached the Lagos office, they seemed barely interested. The heavily built manager was conspicuously lacking in the polished charm of educated Nigerians and his manner left open the possibility that he had not even been expecting me. His precise words were:

'What exactly do you want to do here?'

'Well, I thought the London office told you. I've come to see people from a few ministries, then some shipping agents in Port Harcourt and then I think the plan is that you are going to take me up over the border into Niger.' He looked at his secretary without smiling, spoke in Yoruba and then left the room.

A few minutes later he returned and asked brusquely how much money I had with me.

'Why do you ask?'

'You need money in Nigeria.'

'OK. Seven hundred and fifty dollars.'

'That won't get you much. The Transport Ministry will be two hundred dollars and Finance three hundred dollars.'

'But you can finance me, they told me in London.'

'Did they?'

'Yes… maybe we should ring them… Can we get them on the phone?'

'That'd be difficult: the phones are down at the moment.' It turned out to be true. There were no mobile phones in 1988 and landlines in Nigeria never worked.

'But we'll see what we can do with the ministries,' he conceded.

That day and the next nothing happened, and I sat in a dingy room with nothing to do. Why was I so concerned about not being able to do a good job? Perhaps because I had only been a freelance for a short time. I should have been demanding a ticket home.

It was late in the afternoon of one of the worst days of my life that the door opened and in walked two absurdly sleek young men. Olive skinned, with lustrous longish hair, they might have been models for the Out of Africa clothes that were fashionable in Europe that year.

'Well, great to meet you. Welcome to Lagos. David's told us about you. So how's it going? Everything OK so far?' Georges and Christian were Lebanese, from the Beirut office.

I closed the door and told them how it was going. They looked at each other, rolled their eyes skywards and shook their heads, speaking rapidly in French. Then, back in English, Georges said, 'Look, we're really sorry about this.'

An hour later – some of it spent on a black slab of a walkie-talkie machine and some on a landline that did work – Georges had sorted it out.

'OK, it's all arranged. We get you the meetings with the ministries, then one of our people will take you to Port Harcourt and then another will take you up to the Niger border. By the way, you'll meet up with an Alex MacDonald in Niger. I think you know him.' I seemed to have known Alex for a hundred years.

Three days later I was on the road between Lagos and Port Harcourt, with the Turk. I never quite caught his name. He had been in Nigeria for twenty years. A quietly composed man in his late forties, with an unsmiling manner but a deeply dry sense of humour, he had run large construction projects all over the country and was clearly capable of looking after himself. As we drove along the highway towards the border through dense jungle drenched in tropical rain, he reclined in the back seat, and told me about how things worked in what is most corrupt country in Africa. He said that he welcomed the break from the chaos of Lagos.

All went well until we crossed the state border from Lagos into the state of Bendel. The Turk called it cowboy country, and it was only one mile over the border that we saw our first roadblock, Nigerian style. Lying across the road were two thick planks, penetrated by about a hundred six-inch nails, pointing upwards. We stopped the car, and from behind a tree trooped about ten young men. They signalled to us to wind down the window, and we were addressed by a well-dressed spokesman with heavily exaggerated charm.

'Good afternoon, gentlemen.' His voice was deep and confident. 'I welcome you to the state of Bendel and trust that you are having a pleasant journey... I wonder, however, if I could just check whether you have paid your licence fee for your car radio?'

The driver said yes and showed his receipt.

'Ah, yes, but unfortunately this is the fee paid to the Lagos licensing authority. While here you have to pay to the Bendel authority... Well, you know this is a VERY serious offence...' There followed a short silence. Then he resumed:

'We should strictly be accompanying you to the local police station, but maybe as an alternative you might like to give a small contribution to our local community fund.'

The Turk, who had been looking unperturbed during this exchange, silently put his hand in his pocket, and handed them a few notes. 'That is *very* kind,' the community leader beamed. The planks were hauled to one side and they waved us through, wishing us a good journey.

This happened six times in the next twenty miles. The amount given depended on the degree of menace, which varied in each case. On the sixth occasion, the leader of the welcoming party was about 6'4", foul-mouthed and visibly psychotic. He screamed in the driver's face, spraying him with spit, then opened the door and pulled him out by his neck. For the first time I saw the Turk pale slightly, and a large donation was volunteered. We carried on in silence. He did not speak, and looked fixedly ahead. I asked him if he had been frightened. He didn't turn to look at me: he kept looking ahead, and said, 'Yes.' By early evening we reached the Port Harcourt Hotel.

The most memorable entrance I ever saw occurred in the patio bar at the Port Harcourt Hotel swimming pool. The girl was a prostitute by profession. First to enter were two high-slung battleship breasts, apparently in mid-air. There followed a brief gap, and then the initial sight of the slow-moving, heavy hips – swaying, dipping, undulating in several separate but exquisitely synchronised orbits below a slender waist. Next, the whole body sashayed into view, articulated into interlocking and slowly revolving sections – legs, hips, waist and breasts suspended from broad, powerful shoulders. But the full impact was delayed until the appearance of her neck and head – held high, proud and predatory. Pure witch queen, eyes rolling in an absurd caricature of sensuality, her imperial bearing crowned by a knot of scarlet and dark green bandanas piled up above her head, superb against the deep brown skin. She stopped – arrogant, poised – and surveyed the surrounding tables. Her eyes turned slowly, swivelling like a gun turret rounding on its target. They fixed for a second on mine. I felt like helpless prey, a timid stewpot missionary, but her gaze had already swept elsewhere. With an almost imperceptible shrug of her powerful hips she resumed her progress around the pool, and took her place at a table with two other girls. The rest of the guests turned back to their conversations.

I sat with the Turk over a drink. Like every man in the bar our eyes drifted continually towards the girls. Each and every glance in their direction generated an instant response, the girls' antennae enabling them to lock into immediate eye contact. They held your eye until you returned to your conversation.

The Turk left to go to the toilet, and two girls materialised instantly at our table. They were almost as striking as the witch queen, and went straight into overdrive flirtation. I said that we were busy today, but assured them that maybe tomorrow... When the Turk returned they retreated to their table.

The mistake I had made was not to conceal the number on my room key. So half an hour later, when I had barely returned to my room, there was a knock. I opened the door and there was one of the girls who had come to the table. She had a wide smile, enormous teeth, sensual pneumatic lips and technicolour makeup, looking more formidable than cheap.

'Can I come in?' she said. I made a second mistake, saying I was busy just at the moment, underrating her facility with English.

'What? SO-O-O busy you can't leave it for an hour to enjoy yourself?'

Her theatrical look of incredulity implied that the white man's priorities were beyond laughable. On the other coast of Africa they call the white man a *muzungu*, which means a busy bee, rushing around with his little bits of paper. I carried on the banter but felt pale in the glare of her presence. She seemed to give up, but then tried one final gambit.

'OK... but could you do me a little favour: it's really hot; could I just come in for a quick shower?'

All this time her foot was planted in the door, and her face was a few inches away, her eyes level with mine. She was powerfully built, about cruiserweight, and it dawned on me that she might actually be physically stronger than I was. I wracked my brains for an escape route, but without success, until a group of Dutch sailors arrived in the corridor and she transferred her attention.

I was handed over to my Lebanese protector for the last lap in Kaduna, where he had lived for many years. I spotted him standing outside as we drove up to his house. He was wearing a smart yellow shirt with a little crocodile badge and well pressed brown trousers, and had a neat short haircut. I am sure he knew how to look after himself in Kaduna, but it turned out that he rarely left the city, and once off his own territory, he became increasingly uneasy. He missed his wife and small daughter, and had a wallet full of photographs. His favourite picture, which he showed me often, was of his son and daughter standing with wan smiles in a sunlit back yard in Kaduna. She was about eight and, with her aquiline nose, beaky appearance, a yellow bow in her long dark curls and a shiny satin pink dress, she looked out of place and uncomfortable. The boy was smaller and was wearing a little bow tie.

It soon became clear that rather than his looking after me, the reverse might be the case. He seemed pleased to have a stranger to talk to, to confide in about life's disappointments. Two pieces of information he divulged, and repeated many times, were 'Life is tirribil,' and 'A reech man, he can leeve anywhere and be happy.' But most of all, he feared 'those girls'. Sitting in an open-air bar on the first evening, he lowered his voice and disclosed to me the fundamental difference between the young African girls sitting there, aged thirteen and upwards, mostly in tight white jeans, and girls in Europe or at home.

'The European girls,' he told me, 'will sleep with you, up to a point. But... these girls here... they want NOTHING except sex, and ALL the time!'

He seemed to blench as he contemplated the fate that could befall him if he let his guard drop.

The journey to the border of Niger took two days. By the second day, we had left any connection with Western life far behind; we drove for 300 miles without passing a shop or a restaurant.

Fifty miles before the border, we were stopped by five soldiers. They were about seventeen years old, armour-plated with muscle, bull-necked, heavily armed – and drunk. One waved his gun vaguely in our direction and told us to get out of the car. His eyes were dead, like clouded glass, not quite human. His dress was superficially smart, but deeply grunge in the detail.

'Passport, white man,' he grunted. He looked blearily and unsteadily at it, sneered and dropped it into a ditch. Then they went into a huddle about what to do with us, looking up at us from time to time.

I once knew a very insecure man whose reason for wanting to marry was that he feared falling sick in his flat and not being discovered until after he died. This was the first and only time a similar thought occurred to me. Nobody, absolutely nobody, had any idea of where we were: it would take weeks after our disappearance for anyone to get close to the trail. Maybe the ticket really *was* going to be one way. How could I ever have agreed to it?

The soldiers in their huddle seemed not to be reaching any conclusion. I suddenly heard myself say in a clear voice:

'Can we have our passports back?'

The leader looked distracted and confused by a question he had not expected. He hesitated. I went on, 'Is there a problem?' to keep the initiative. Then I manufactured what I hoped looked like a big smile. He seemed to puzzle for a second, and then turned away and grunted assent. We picked the passports out of the ditch, got into the car and drove off, too drained to speak.

We drove for another fifty miles, and crossed the border into Niger and on to Niamey, the capital. As we approached the hotel, I spotted Alex sitting reading on a balcony. I shouted up at him. For a few seconds he said nothing, just grinned with a look that said 'What on earth are we doing here?'

'You won't believe it,' he shouted down, 'but they've got some shortbread biscuits here. Come up and have a nice cup of tea.' More or less unchanged, Alex was still the son of a Scottish Presbyterian minister, although now a little more louche. He had worked in twenty-five African countries, and had once been married to the formidable madam of a bar in one of them.

Niamey was quiet, formal and dull. It had a French town hall, a library, an Alliance Francaise and a museum. Within a day I was missing Nigeria.

E T Laing was born in Northern Ireland, brought up in Newcastle-on-Tyne, educated at Oxford University and lives in London with his family. He works mainly in aid to developing countries and when it dawned on him that it had taken him to at least seventy countries it seemed a dereliction  of duty not to write about them. His travel book, *Fakirs, Feluccas and Femmes Fatales*, from which the above story was adapted, was published by Bradt in 2012. He continues to work around the world, adding to his list of countries.

Close Encounter
with an Elephant
Brian Jackman

It was the late 1970s and I was still new to Africa when I flew to Zambia to write a travel feature for *The Sunday Times* on Kafue, a remote national park the size of Wales.

My guide was Cecil Evans, a former park warden who was built like a baobab tree and known as Nyama Yangu (My Meat) due to his reputation for chasing lions off zebra kills and taking home a choice cut for his Sunday lunch.

We met at an unpretentious safari lodge on the shores of Itezhi-Tezhi, a huge artificial lake created by the damming of the Kafue River, and set off in his Land Rover, pursued by clouds of tsetse flies that forced us to keep the windows closed as we tried in vain to outpace them.

Eventually we parked the vehicle and set off on foot into the bush. Although I had been on a walking safari on a previous visit to Zambia this was still a novel experience and I was relieved to see that Cecil carried a rifle. Kafue in those days was still totally wild, a vast mosaic of floodplains, teak forests and crackling dry *miombo* woodland alive with lion, buffalo – and elephant.

Walking releases you from the tyranny of roads. On foot you are free to interpret the calligraphy of animal tracks laid out in the dust, to hear every sound and catch the scent of sun-dried grass. Only with your boots on the ground do you meet Africa on level terms, and the thought of coming face to face with one of the Big Five as we tiptoed through the ten-foot-tall adrenalin grass reawakened senses I never knew I possessed.

We walked in silence, Cecil in front, cradling his rifle as he scanned the bush from side to side. At one point we came upon lion tracks, each broad print the size of my hand, but they were several days old, said Cecil.

At this point I began to relax, think less about running into a buffalo bull and concentrate instead on trying to unravel the continual soundtrack of bird calls: the insane braying of hornbills, the fluting duets of black-collared barbets and the Cape turtledoves exhorting Africa to 'work-harder, work-harder'.

Soon afterwards, having been walking for just over an hour, we came upon a pack of wild dogs, the painted wolves of Africa, which ran down and killed a grysbok right in front of us. From a distance we watched them demolish the carcass in a matter of minutes, and when they had trotted off through the grass we, too, resumed our journey.

As the sun rose higher, the day grew hotter and the tsetse continued to bite us remorselessly. In a little while we came to a wood at the edge of the plains, when suddenly and without any warning a very large bull elephant exploded from the trees and came straight for us – six tons of unconstrained fury, screaming like an express train. 'Stand still, don't run,' said Cecil, a singularly worthless piece of advice since an elephant can move faster than Usain Bolt, and in any case my legs had turned to jelly.

Cecil stepped forward, slapping the butt of his gun and shouting obscenities at the angry tusker, which skidded to a halt just a few metres in front of us, shaking its huge ragged ears as it towered over us, blotting out the sky.

There followed a brief but nail-biting stand-off which ended only when Cecil took off his bush hat and hurled it at the elephant, screaming 'Bugger off' at the top of his voice, upon which the big bull span round and lumbered back into the bush from where it had come, ripping a sapling out of the ground as it did so.

Had we faced down a mock charge or been confronted by the real thing? I had read about mock charges – the threat displays that elephants sometimes perform to intimidate potential aggressors – and remembered the words of Ian Douglas-Hamilton, the world's leading authority on elephant behaviour. 'An elephant's mock charge is meant to impress you,' he told me. 'They've spent millions of years perfecting it.'

But this was different. Cecil knew that, and I could sense it, too. I had the distinct feeling it would have loved nothing better than to scoop me up in its thick yellow tusks and hurl me over the nearest acacia, or else stamp me into an unrecognisable pulp.

Had this bull been pursued recently by ivory poachers? Or was he in the condition known as *musth* – pumped up with testosterone for the breeding season? Certainly the temporal glands on either side of his head were streaming – a sure sign of stress. But whatever the reason for his bad temper he seemed intent on taking it out on us, and it was simply our bad luck to be in the wrong place at the wrong time.

Afterwards, in a silence broken only by the mindless chanting of doves in the woodlands, I wiped the sweat from my face and waited for my heartbeat to fall back to normal while Cecil retrieved his hat. 'Welcome to Kafue,' he said.

Brian Jackman is best known as Britain's foremost writer on African wildlife safaris. For twenty years he worked for *The Sunday Times*, and was voted Travel Writer of the Year in 1982. Today his work appears mostly in *The Daily Telegraph*, *BBC Wildlife*  magazine and *Travel Africa*. His African books include *Roaring at the Dawn*, *The Marsh Lions* and *The Big Cat Diary* (both with Jonathan Scott), and most recently Bradt's *Savannah Diaries*.

The Virtue of Ignorance
Tim Cahill

For reasons that remain opaque, the United States State Department recently chose me to give a series of lectures in the country of Georgia. I understood that I was representing America and tried hard to be a good ambassador.

'How do you like our country?' the television reporters wanted to know. It was the most asked question of my trip. 'The food is superb,' I said, 'the wine is excellent, the people hospitable and the mountains and rivers and ancient monasteries and battlements are soul stirring.' I had several variations of this sentiment memorised and I was able to say each of them with a great deal of enthusiasm because it was all true.

The Georgians I met – mostly university folk: American Studies professors and students – were intent on their own questions. One of which was, of course, 'what do you, as an American, think of our country?'

Most of the people I spoke with seemed pleased with my impressions. Smiles all around. I accepted invitations to *supras*, elaborate dinners (Thanksgiving comes to mind) that might include roast suckling pig, chopped spinach and walnuts, along with many varieties of cheese and bread, all washed down with the excellent, earthy wines. As is the custom, a toastmaster (*tomada*) proposed toasts to all present, then, in separate toasts that continued throughout dinner, to those who couldn't come, to those who have passed before, and to new friends (me). The toasts were lengthy, elaborate and emotional. I was welcomed not just into Georgia, but into the family. Seldom have I felt so honoured.

But frankly, I have not always been a credit to my country while travelling and have committed any number of idiocies abroad.

Most of them were due to simple ignorance. For example, at one time I did not know the Burundi National Anthem. This is of some importance if you happen to be in Burundi, loading a bush plane, and one of the songs playing on the scratchy sounding loudspeakers at the airport happens to be the National Anthem. If you know the song, you stand to attention. And if you don't, a soldier will escort you to the broom closet where you will sit for a couple of hours learning respect.

My travels over the past forty years have featured a rather astounding number of boneheaded faux pas. On my way to visit Iran's historic Valley of the Assassins, I found myself sitting in a bus, trying to communicate with a number of Iranian men who'd ascertained that I was from America and had taken a keen interest in me. I wanted to tell them that, while our respective governments were sometimes at odds, friendship between the people of America and the people of Iran was a real good idea. However, I was entirely innocent of Farsi and tried to express this concept as if in a game of charades. One of the gestures I used was a big smile with both thumbs up. All the Iranians around me returned the smile and gave me the thumbs up. There was even a bit of laughter. I was a funny guy. The Iranians liked me. I'd made my point.

Unfortunately, I later discovered that, in Iran, the thumbs-up gesture means almost exactly the opposite of what it means in the US. So what I said to my new Iranian friends was, 'Up yours.' And they all replied, 'And up yours too, buddy.'

On other occasions, I have been detained and questioned simply because the local authorities suspected my mission was nefarious in nature. This generally happens in very remote areas where people aren't used to Americans and assume we didn't walk all those miles for nothing. In the cloud forests of Peru, where I was searching for pre-Columbian ruins, the local Peruvian Investigative Police (PIP) officer called our group in for a three-hour chat.

He wondered if we might be, oh, peeking into graves up there in the ruins. He took us through a room with materials the PIP had confiscated. Among the items were a few metal trinkets and some metal detectors taken from captured grave robbers. Who were now, the officer assured us, in jail for a very long time. He said that if we were innocent, we surely wouldn't mind if he searched through our backpacks. For buried treasures. Or metal detectors. Instead, he got the dirty socks of innocence.

In Tonga, where I was studying the life cycle of giant clams with a prominent scientist, the people of the village thought we were figuring out some way to make money off the creatures and cheat them out of their birthright. I tried to explain the scientist was, in fact, trying to find ways to conserve the population. I talked with people in bars and even at church services I attended for the purpose. In all cases, I was greeted with polite disbelief. A bad ambassador, I'm afraid.

Ignorance has served me well only once. Turkish police detained me and my friends at a number of successive roadblocks in the southeast portion of the country. They did not believe that I was searching for the supposedly extinct Caspian tiger. To them, I was likely one of those journalists who was going to write a story about how badly Turks treated the Kurds who lived there. Roadblock conduct requires that all necessary documents be produced promptly. Soon enough, if the papers are in order, it is time to joke with the police. We'd have a good chance of passing through into the tiger's territory if we could get them laughing. And we had a ready fire knee-slapper right there on my passport. My first name, Tim, could be Timur, a common Turkish name referring to the fifteenth-century Turko-Mongol conqueror, Tamerlane or Timur the Lame.

It was my last name that got them laughing. Cahill looks much like the word 'cahil,' which in Turkish means 'ignorant.' Timur the Ignorant. It was like being called Attila the Jerk. The officers laughed and laughed. But they let us through. And so, in this case, ignorance worked in my favour.

I can't say I will never again be detained or questioned or that I won't embarrass myself in some cultural gaffe. Travel is a process of learning what you don't know. And sometimes you have to learn the hard way.

The Georgians, I suspect, have a toast for that. 'To the ignorance that propels us into knowledge. Cheers.' No wait. Kill the 'cheers.' It is considered slightly inappropriate to say while toasting in Georgia. I learned that the hard way.

Tim Cahill is an American writer and founding editor of *Outside* magazine. He has won the National Magazine Award and is the author of nine books and several documentary IMAX screenplays, two of which were nominated for an Academy Award.

Tak Jadi

Jude Marwa

Can't be bothered today, I thought, as I walked straight past the long pre-paid taxi queue. I'll book one myself. I dug around in my bag for my phone. Typical. No credit. So I headed for the 7-Eleven in departures.

Walking out of arrivals I winced as the damp, warm air of KL engulfed me. Sweat was soon pouring off me. Before I reached the shop, the horrific sound of an engine that had to be falling out caught my attention. A battered old Proton taxi pulled up and a man got out. The driver fetched his suitcase from the boot. I hesitated. It wasn't registered, but it was available. I made a beeline for it and with a nod from the driver I dived into the back seat, relishing the crisp coolness from the aircon.

'Desa Parkcity, Kepong please... on meter.'

'Yes ma'am. Your first time here ma'am?'

'No, I live here, been here two years now.'

'You have children?'

'Yeah I've got two. And you?'

'Yes ma'am, two boys, four years, six years.'

'Ah, bet they keep you busy!'

'Oh yes ma'am they very busy yes ma'am, but wife she wants girl. You – boys?'

'I have one girl and one boy.'

'Oh lucky, yes?'

'Sometimes... sometimes not!' I laughed.

Relaxed, I closed my eyes and rested my head against the cool glass of the window.

A while later I awoke and looked around for the familiar landmark of the Petronas Towers. There they were – behind me? That wasn't right. I was confused. I leant forward so the driver could hear me over the drone of the engine.

'This isn't the route I usually take.'

No answer. I raised my voice.

'I haven't been this way before, you sure you know the way?'

'Yes ma'am... other way much traffic.'

The driver looked back at me in his mirror. Our eyes met and his darted away. I started to feel uneasy.

'This doesn't lead to Desa Park, can you turn round please, this is the wrong way.'

There was no response. I glared in the mirror willing him to look back at me, but instead he stared ahead, stony faced.

I felt panic seep into my body.

Looking around the taxi for some peace of mind I noticed his ID taped to the dashboard. I grappled with my ego, stupidity and regret momentarily before taking my phone out. My only hope was to pretend. So I spoke into the dead line.

'Hi, yes I'm in a cab but he's not taking me home. I don't know where he is taking me. His name is Lee Hong and his number is RK522340. Yeah, you can track me on your iPhone. Yeah, I'll stay on the phone.'

I clocked the driver looking at me again. I hardened my gaze. We turned off the highway as he drove at speed into a village and took another left. We were heading towards jungle. I tried the handle on the door, ready to make a run for it, but it wouldn't budge.

We took a final bend and I saw ahead what I had feared but not allowed myself to fully believe. Four men stood at the roadside facing the taxi. We began to slow. My heart raced. I gave one last pointless piece of information to my fictional rescuer on the phone.

'I think he's delivering me to some men. I think I'm being sold.'

I felt a tear roll down my face. This was it. The end of everything I knew, my life about to become something people read about.

The taxi pulled up, the engine still running. I felt my chest rise, my throat tighten. More tears fell. The car echoed with the sound of my breath.

I watched the driver wipe beads of sweat from his eyes as he wound down the window of his battered old Proton.

'*Tak jadi! Tak jadi!*'

The men looked at each other. One stepped forward and booted the driver's door with his foot.

I let out a yelp.

'*Tak jadi...* Can't lah, won't work.' His voice broke.

He cowered, and began to ramble, desperation oozing out of every word. Another of the group stepped forward and grabbed his face.

Then I heard a word I understood.

'Tracker.'

The men stopped shouting and looked at me.

My phone was in my hand.

Before I knew what was happening the gang had mounted their bikes and they were gone.

The driver and I were left with the overpowering din of the engine and the smell of our sweat: frozen in a moment of cascading emotions. I needed to get out. As I reached for the door handle again the driver reached for his, tripping on the lip of the door in his scramble. I felt fear and panic inside of me as he yanked open my door yelling, '*Get out!!*' I too stumbled, frantically trying to get away. I started to run down the track towards the *kampong*. I glanced back to see him drag my bag out. I kept running, listening to the fading sound of his dying engine. Silence. I looked up to see I was almost at the kampong and a familiar red advertising board with Maxi in large white letters was right there. For the first time ever I read their slogan: recharge reload mobile Malaysia.

Facing a pregnant lady, I held it together for long enough to say, 'Thirty ringgit top up please.'

Collapsing down on a step I punched the PIN into my phone and called my husband. With kampong life carrying on around me I lay my head on my knees and cried.

Jude Marwa is from the UK, and this story was shortlisted for the Bradt/ *Independent on Sunday* Travel Writing Competition. She currently lives and works in Kuala Lumpur with her family, and is writing her first novel. She shares some of her touching,  funny and precarious anecdotes on her aptly titled blog, 'Shambolic Expats': http://judemarwa.blogspot.com/

Commando Raid

John Harrison

In 1979, when I travelled by steamer down the Rio Madeira, the cargo of live turtles grew at every stop. Passengers embarked with them as extra luggage, or men paddled out and sold them to the captain. Soon even the floor space under the hammocks had its cargo of mute suffering. Laid on their backs, they were rendered helpless, undignified and pitiful. They waved their legs, extended their grandfatherly necks and spent the journey trying to right themselves. Very occasionally one would succeed if its legs could get a purchase, and many had their legs tied tightly across the underside of the shell to prevent this.

Many had been caught weeks before and kept in pens waiting for the steamer to arrive, with no food or water. Turtles can live for much longer without sustenance, so it was deemed unnecessary. Several had the puncture hole of the harpoon in the carapace, which oozed a watery blood. Very soon nearly all had rubbed raw patches in their legs and necks from chafing against their inverted shells. Others had bleeding wounds from the cords that tied their legs.

There was only one other gringo on board, an American, who viewed the pitiful cargo with even more outrage than I. We remonstrated with the passengers and the captain that the creatures should be watered and fed, kept untethered in the hold, should not be taken in September when some of the captives were undoubtedly egg-carrying females. All to no avail.

If we'd been richer we might have bought the lot and released them – but from talking to the passengers we realised we'd have to be rich indeed. Every kilometre nearer to Manaus their value increased. Turtles are a delicacy and everyone was going to profit from their sale, especially the captain, who had purchased several dozen.

The idea of a commando raid to release the prisoners came to us one night as we lay side by side in our hammocks passing a bottle of *cachaça* between us.

Cachaça is a fiery cane spirit that has to be tossed back and gulped with a fair amount of grimacing and exhaled breath. Once inside, however, it makes the stomach glow, the coward brave, the meek proud, the proud unbearable, the uncertain resolute and the cautious reckless. It made us embark on a foolhardy mission while the other passengers lay snoring in their hammocks with only the pilot awake at the wheel on the upper deck. We flitted about on our bare feet, shivering in the 2 a.m. chill, running our hands over the turtles' shells checking for harpoon punctures. Any without, we untied, carried to the rail and dropped overboard.

It took only half an hour and in that time we liberated sixty or seventy. That was only about a third of the total, but there seemed no point in releasing the wounded ones, and I think we hoped that no-one would notice any were missing.

Some hope. By the time we awoke, hung-over and exhausted by our nocturnal mission, it was very clear that bad feeling was afoot.

Every visitor to Brazil comments on the gentleness and charm of the average Brazilian. They are a warm-hearted, easy-going, amusing race, welcoming to foreigners. Well, I can assure you that they had undergone a transformation on that particular boat. Until we got to Manaus the atmosphere was distinctly uncomfortable. Everyone stared at us with murder in their eyes, and the American and I took it in turns to go to sleep. No-one voiced an accusation. Not once. But people would get up and eat elsewhere when we sat next to them at meals; stop talking when we approached; spit pointedly when we leant on the rail near them.

As for us, we felt a mixture of guilt and glee. We had deprived some poor people of a deserved addition to their meagre income – but we had thrown overboard three-quarters of the captain's personal cargo and he could afford the loss. We felt that self-righteous, persecuted glow of reformers and once we got off the boat we had no doubt we'd done the right thing.

John Harrison hitchhiked from London to Johannesburg before he was twenty-one, and after two further years hitching around every country in South and Central America, he never really shook off the travel bug. He has written and presented radio programmes for the BBC, contributed articles to magazines and newspapers, and entertained audiences with more than 200 lectures over the last twenty-five years, including work as an on-board speaker for cruise lines. He lives in Bristol, where he has his own construction company, and is the author of *Into the Amazon* and Bradt's *Up The Creek*, of which this is an extract.

Eyes Closed, Full Speed Ahead
Claire Morsman

The searing temperatures of the mid-Australian outback sap my energy. Distance has taken on a whole different meaning and although the Stuart Highway stretches ad infinitum, seemingly an unchallenging drive, the monotony of the featureless landscape and intense heat throws down its gauntlet. The endless pink-hued tarmac hums beneath my tyres, soporifically willing me to let my eyes close.

Just for a moment. Close.

Alone in a slow-cooking van of the very highest backpacker quality, I put another tape into the slot, all windows wound down flush to the bodywork, mosquito net flapping like a sail in the back. The vermilion dust all around – on everything I touch, in everything I eat and in every crevice of me and my van.

Sleepy. Close. Just for a second.

I turn the music up higher and ya-hooo out of the window. I pull my head in quickly though, as, in reality, the experience is like staring into a hairdryer, with the setting stuck on 'Too Hot'.

Sleepy. Hot, heavy eyelid rims.

The horizon is always a simmering haze and the road ahead is ruler drawn. I fail to notice the devil's own transport behind me until the roar fills my own vehicle and his chrome bull bars loom through my back window. Fifty metres of road train pass in a shattering rain of dust and pebbledash. The top of his wheels are as high as my roof rack. Shiiiiit!

Go on. Close. One second won't matter. Eyes will feel less itchy and heavy if you do.

I pour some warm water out of a plastic bottle on to my head, rub my eyes, and then see somebody on the barren dust. A hitchhiker. I find it strange to have to drive the van, actually slow down, change gear and stop.

He is scruffy, Irish and bothered by the flies. I pull my shirt away from my sticky back. Off again. Soon, I notice his eyes closing and catch him looking longingly at the mattress in the back.

'I'm knackered,' he says. 'I'd be more help if I get some kip now and drive later on. Refreshed like.'

'Fine,' I nod, inwardly un-fine.

Closey closey eyes. Go on...

A terrible stench fills the van. The hellish aroma wakes me up. We whizz past a swollen bull, inflated like a Goodyear blimp and heinously rotting in the heat. Nightmarish birds hover for a feed. Entirely awake now, my right arm burnt to a crisp to match the outback hues, I notice black clouds on the horizon. Rain? Surely not. The cloud is moving fast and I anticipate the novel movement of flicking the windscreen wiper switch – until I smell the smoke.

As acrid as the decomposing innards of the bull that came off second best to a road train; yet this smell is different. It's the wafting stink of impending death to all those who cannot run fast enough. I consult my rear-view mirror, hoping that this might be the moment when my co-pilot snaps into action. What happens in a bush fire exactly? Everything burns! Calm. It's a long way away yet.

Unlike any other outback vista, a wall of fire moves bloody quickly. I call out. 'Ahem, hello! Jeff, er Julian.' What is his name? 'Christ!' The flame is gorging on the scrub to the left of us. Surely we'll be fine? It's all around! It's on the road! The ROAD is burning! Smoke is stinging and blinding my eyes, by now ineffectually wide with terror. Sleep, except for the eternal kind, is now far from my mind.

'The tyres are melting!' I scream in absolute sheer panic. I feel the van give in to the sluggish pull of the bubbling tarmac. My feet are bare. I'll burn to death if I leave the van; I'll burn to death if I stay put. We're slowing. My hot tears of panic help clear smoke from my eyes and then I feel a hand on my shoulder.

'Let her out!' his accent commands. I push my foot down and we surge forward, hurtling through the wall of all-consuming flames. His voice murmurs, 'Now we're sucking diesel,' as he turns back round to find a comfortable spot to sleep again.

Rigid with shock, I drive until we reach a feral outpost. The wheels hadn't been melting. It'd been the crackling inferno surrounding us that had sounded like burning rubber. We stop. My unflustered, well-rested companion climbs out. He mentions that the fire had been good craic. Would I like him to drive for a bit?

I move into the back and find that I can't sleep. Eventually I push the visions of death by incineration to the back of my mind and persuade my eyes to *close*, the endless pink-hued tarmac humming beneath the tyres.

Claire Morsman travels extensively for both work and pleasure, and is nearly always moved to write about it. The above story was shortlisted for the Bradt/*Independent on Sunday* Travel Writing Competition in 2012. She is an international English examiner,  professional declutterer, Moroccan guesthouse owner, teacher, animal lover and morsbag maker. She is always looking forward to visiting somewhere new, and often longing to revisit somewhere she's already been. As long as she's on the move, she's happy.

Pavel and the Beige Fleece
Lyn Hughes

'Star jump, star jump, star JUMP!' I muttered to myself as motivation, desperately trying to warm myself up on a sub-zero night in the high steppes of Kyrgyzstan.

I'd been proud of being able to travel light when my guide had met me at Bishkek Airport, forty-eight hours earlier. 'Where's the rest of your luggage?' Pavel had asked, looking quizzically at my bag which was clearly only half-full. 'That's it!' I'd responded proudly. I didn't feel so smug now.

In truth, I hadn't intended to travel quite so scantily. I'd been frantically busy in the lead-up to the trip, and hadn't looked at the itinerary and packing list provided by a specialist tour operator. Running late on the day of departure I had pulled on my walking boots, thrown a few vitals into my bag and headed for the airport.

My one bit of research had been to look up the weather in Bishkek, and it forecast temperatures in the mid to high 30s for the following few days. So, I bought three t-shirts at Heathrow, and figured I was sorted.

Bishkek in mid-July was indeed hot and humid. We spent a day visiting its sights and then drove out the next morning by Land Cruiser to spend a week exploring.

Taking a winding road up into the mountains, I started to recall being told that Kyrgyzstan is crammed with lakes and mountains. Indeed, the 'Mountains of Heaven' – the Tian Shan – extend the length of the country, and more than ninety per cent of Kyrgyzstan is higher than 1,500 metres.

We climbed higher and higher, past soaring golden eagles, and started to come across patches of snow. We pulled over at one point, and had a quick snowball fight, before entering the high grasslands surrounding Lake Song-Köl, glittering a glacial blue in front of us. Yurt camps were scattered over the plateau, wisps of smoke feathering up towards the clear sky.

After another hour's drive we pulled up at a camp as dusk fell. I was shown to my yurt – a large circular space, no flooring, just grass, and no furniture; just a mattress and a blanket. By the time I went to bed the temperature had dropped to near freezing and my teeth were chattering. I began to curse not having brought warm clothing with me – the only things I had with long sleeves were a light sweatshirt and an even lighter unlined jacket.

Piling on every item of clothing I had, I snuggled under the blanket. But I woke again in the early hours, stiff from the cold. I got up and jogged on the spot, windmilled my arms, and then settled on star jumps as the most effective way to warm myself up.

The spine-tingling call of a wolf echoed through the valley, setting off hysterical barking from every dog for miles around. More wolves howled, joining the chorus, before they moved away and a deep silence returned.

Two hours later, and worn out after my exertions, I ventured out of my yurt to a crunchy frost coating the ground. A patient-looking black horse was waiting nearby to take me for a pre-breakfast ride. We set off down the valley to the lake, which was shimmering turquoise blue in the early morning sun, and had a mosey along the shore before trotting back up the valley.

By the time I arrived back at camp, I was warm enough that I could take off my sweatshirt and jacket. We were leaving after breakfast, so I got my bag from the yurt and left it by the car, dropping my discarded clothing on it while I grabbed some food, and then gave a goodbye pat to Kashka the horse.

Retracing our route back along the lake, we pulled in at another yurt camp, where Pavel's girlfriend – also a guide – was staying with her clients. To my surprise, who should those clients be but someone I knew from the UK, the boss of a well-respected travel company, and his girlfriend.

Craig beckoned me into his yurt, where he and Joanne were packing their kit. 'We had a disaster,' said Craig. 'One of our bags never arrived so we're missing half our luggage.' I sympathised as they explained how short they were on underwear, and were having to share what they had.

But what they did have – as well as some bottles of red wine – were proper, big technical jackets, and four-season sleeping bags. 'We didn't half have to bring a lot of kit,' he said. It finally dawned on me that I was woefully underprepared.

Having said our goodbyes, we carried on for several hours to our next stop. The driver unloaded the car. 'Where's my jacket?' I asked. Pavel and the driver looked mystified. I had already been dreading the cold nights ahead. Now, my heart sank as I realised that my only item of long-sleeved clothing had somehow gone missing, presumably at the yurt camp a couple of hundred miles away.

Pavel was travelling light himself, but he had both a fleece and a rain jacket and now gave me the choice – I could borrow one or the other for the rest of my trip. Hating the cold, and being tired of star jumps, I went for the beige-coloured fleece.

Pavel assured me that he was used to the temperatures. And this, after all, was summer, so he'd be fine. I knew he was making light of it, and was probably cursing my irresponsibility. But that fleece was to be a lifesaver, being cosier than the clothing I had lost. And whenever I got to a yurt camp, I would ask for two mattresses, putting one on top of the other to keep me warm underneath, and would beg several blankets.

The night-time strategy worked until we crossed the border into Kazakhstan to spend the night at a basecamp for the high peaks of the central Tian Shan. Set on a windswept plateau just below the snowline, the tented village hosted a transient population of mountaineers and high-altitude hikers.

I was shown to a small A-frame tent with nothing in it. I sought out the camp manager and explained that I had no sleeping bag. He looked me up and down, taking in the lack of layers, and told me that they didn't provide bedding. All around fit-looking types were striding around in Michelin-man jackets, overtrousers, mittens and beanie hats.

A long building housed a dining room and, even better, a cosy bar, with warming Kazakh brandy at US$1 a shot. Dreading having to go to the tent, I prayed the bar would stay open all night. Pavel felt duty-bound to stay with me as I lingered over my drinks, desperately keeping a conversation going. I saw poor Pavel fighting to keep his eyes open as the hours dawdled by. Eventually, there were only the two of us left in the bar, and the barman had stacked the empty chairs on to the tables around us. I had to give in and leave the warmest place I'd been for days.

The next day, we headed for the east of Kyrgyzstan and the natural wonders of Jeti-Öghüz Canyon. This was the bit of the itinerary that Pavel had been really looking forward to. Primarily a mountain guide, he was excited about sharing his favourite area of his country with me. I, on the other hand, was feeling increasingly apprehensive about exploring mountains in little more than a borrowed fleece.

We arrived on a Sunday, and the beautiful but rainswept valley was scattered with bedraggled picnicking families, huddled under the tractor-driven wagons they had arrived on.

At the yurt camp that would be our base for the next couple of nights we gratefully accepted bowls of hot tea. The low table was laid in typical style with dried fruit and nuts, jam and bowls of sweets. Tea led on to an excellent three-course dinner, shared with a party of lively Norwegians, all bundled up in ski and mountain-wear, and their plentiful supply of vodka.

The next morning I woke with a hangover to the patter of rain, and the surrounding peaks were hidden by swirling mists. Pavel was itching to get going on a full day hike that would take us to an amazing view of Öghüz-Bashi, an iconic peak known for its beauty. We grabbed a quick breakfast and set off, hoping that the weather would clear.

The scenery was typically alpine, the meadow scattered with small, colourful wild flowers, while spruce and juniper coated the canyon walls. To our right gushed a fast-flowing river, swollen with the rain. We squelched through bog, passed through a small patch of woodland and, once out in the open again, spotted a yurt set part way up the hillside on which horses grazed.

Smoke rose from the yurt, so we headed up to it, and were invited inside by the welcoming family. There were three generations here: head of the family Toktobai and his wife, Koen, their daughter Nazira and her three children, plus Toktobai's brother. We sat on the floor around the stove, Toktobai taking prime spot. We were offered *kymys* – fermented mares' milk. It tasted like slightly sour yoghurt, nowhere near as fearsome as I'd imagined.

'This is very young,' explained Pavel, sipping it thoughtfully, like a wine connoisseur presented with a glass of Beaujolais. 'Just a day old, I would say.' He turned to the family to have his assumption confirmed.

After two more bowls of kymys we braved the elements to carry on walking. The mountains were still shrouded in low clouds that showed little sign of lifting, and a persistent cold fine rain was falling. I was finding it difficult to go at the same pace as Pavel on the slippery grass, and was demoralised to realise that we had only gone a fraction of the way we had to cover.

Then the drizzle suddenly became a downpour, as if a tap had been turned on. I was quickly soaked through, very cold and very miserable. Even Pavel was shivering, and I felt guilty yet again at having purloined his fleece. While just as guiltily wishing he'd give me his waterproof too. After forty-five minutes I was relieved when he looked back at me and asked whether I wanted to give up. I didn't need to speak. We turned round, the yurt a welcome beacon to aim for.

Despite the rain, the family were outside as it was almost time to milk the mares. The herd was rounded up from the hillside by eighteen-year-old Eldiar and brought down to where their foals were kept tied to a line to prevent the mares from wandering too far.

We huddled back around the wood-burning stove in the yurt, drank more kymys and arranged to hire a couple of horses to take us back to our camp. I clambered on to Eldiar's roan horse while Pavel and Eldiar doubled up on a bay mare.

The horses kept their footing as we weaved our way around boulders and negotiated thick mud and bogs. I clung on to my mount's mane as we cut across a bend in the boulder-strewn river, the horses plunging chest-deep into icy water.

The rain got even heavier, lashing our faces, only to be replaced by driving hailstones, while the rumble of thunder and flashes of lightning accompanied us most of the way. I was soaked through to the bone, my eyes and nose streaming, and my hands blue with cold. But for once on the trip, I felt pure joy. It was exhilarating – I couldn't wipe the grin off my face. And even Pavel was smiling too. We hugged when we got off the horses, bonded at last.

The next evening, back in sultry Bishkek, there was a ceremonial handing back of the now grubby fleece to the long-suffering Pavel. 'I'll never forget this trip,' he said. Oh, so true.

I admitted to him that I had been instrumental in setting up an award scheme for guides – The World Guide Awards – feeling they were not always recognised for their role in creating memorable holidays for their clients. Or appreciated for putting up with stupid clients, I thought.

Lyn Hughes co-founded *Wanderlust* magazine in 1993, having had the idea on a flight to South America when she was travelling hand luggage only for a six-month trip. Since her Kyrgyzstan jaunt she has given up espousing the benefits of travelling light, and has tried to always Be Prepared. As a judge of the World Guide Awards she has developed an even healthier respect for the unsung heroes of travel – guides.

Surviving Life in the Wild
Jonathan and Angela Scott

My wife Angela was born in Africa and from the age of four was raised in Dar es Salaam in Tanzania, growing up on safari: she was already living half my dream. Angela's soul mates were bush babies and mongooses, rich fare compared to the domestic cats and dogs that were my companions as a child in England, though the sudden emergence of a ferret or two from the deep pockets of the local gamekeeper's greatcoat – all fiery-eyed, wraithlike suppleness – certainly added a bit of spice to life on our farm in Berkshire. When I graduated to hamsters and guinea pigs, then slow worms and grass snakes, I thought that was pretty exciting, but by the time I left my home in England forty years ago in search of adventure in Africa, I was dreaming of a life among wild animals – the bigger the better.

Tales of 'derring-do', particularly when played out among large charismatic creatures in the world's wild places, have always found a ready audience, and not just for those living a more sedate urban existence. The film *Born Free* featuring legendary Kenya game warden George Adamson, his eccentric wife Joy and their lioness Elsa certainly caught my attention and fuelled my ambitions growing up in England. So did the popular 1960s TV series *On Safari* featuring the intrepid filmmakers Armand and Michaela Dennis racing around the wilds of Africa in their open-top jeep, bouncing from one near-death experience to another – or so it seemed. But if Angie and I have learned anything from living among large and potentially dangerous wild animals here in Africa, it's that when trouble strikes it is invariably due to ignorance, complacency or incaution on the part of the people involved, igniting the animals' natural defensive response in protecting themselves or their young from real or perceived harm. A leopard wounded by a trophy hunter, a cow elephant anxious for the safety of her young calf or a buffalo surprised in thick bush can all be terrifyingly unforgiving adversaries when they charge towards you. Surviving such an incident is certainly something to write home about and a tasty item for the press.

We have surprised all the large charismatic African animals at close quarters – the lions, leopards, elephants, buffalos, rhinos, hippos (along with a variety of venomous snakes). We have run from feisty hippos in the Mara while listening to them chomping their teeth with displeasure, and a bull elephant called Tyson charged us while filming in Tsavo National Park and trashed US$50,000 of camera equipment as we ran for our lives. Angie nearly sat on a puff adder during a tea break in the bush, while many years earlier I noosed an Egyptian cobra in Botswana with a homemade catching stick that snapped in two, freeing the snake to strike just inches from my face. And then there was the time near Governor's Camp when I unintentionally shared the back seat of our safari vehicle with a large male baboon intent on stealing my treasured bag of crisps and brandishing canines the size of my thumb to intimidate me. All of these incidents were guaranteed to get the adrenalin pumping – and in the main thoroughly avoidable.

But the reality is that it is the little creatures you never see – except perhaps in a biology class or under a microscope in a tropical diseases laboratory – that are most likely to put you in hospital or even kill you. A million people die of malaria in Africa each year, mostly children under the age of five. I contracted my first dose of malaria along with a gut-wrenching bout of amoebic dysentery in 1974 while travelling overland through the Central African Republic and Zaire (now the Democratic Republic of the Congo). If you want to lose a few pounds fast that's the way to do it. Hard as it is, the best defence against malaria is to forgo the more comfortable shorts and sandals for long trousers and socks in the evening, smother yourself with insect repellent and sleep under a well-secured mosquito net treated with repellent. Easy of course in hindsight – we slept under the stars on camp beds, often without mosquito nets or with ones that were woefully inadequate.

Ironically, though, the most frightening incident Angie and I have faced wasn't in Africa at all. It was during one of our many expeditions to Antarctica. The beauty of the frozen south is that most of the creatures you encounter on land are completely unafraid of man. Elephant seals might weigh up to four tons and look pretty fearsome but they mostly slumber like giant slabs of lard along the pebble beaches, while penguins wander up to you confident that you mean them no harm.

The one creature that everyone tells you to be wary of is the Antarctic fur seal – particularly during the breeding season when the testosterone-fuelled males are at their feistiest. This coincides with the Antarctic summer when tourism is at its peak. You only have to watch the rival 'beachmasters', as the mature dominant male fur seals are known, charging across the beaches to compete for the right to mate with females (barely a week after they have given birth) to know that these are animals to be avoided. Unlike true seals that move about like velvety sacks of potatoes, the eared seals comprising the sea lions and fur seals are able to run faster than Usain Bolt. Due to their ability to direct their hind flippers forwards, they can launch themselves towards you at a startling gallop. Add to that a set of teeth to rival a leopard's and you have a 110 kilogram running machine that can tear through human flesh and leave a nasty infected wound. But by listening to sound advice we have always managed to avoid trouble. That is, until we came face to face with a Hooker's sea lion – which looks like a fur seal, but double the size.

We were on a one-month semi-circumnavigation of Antarctica travelling on the *Kapitan Khlebnikov*, the legendary Russian icebreaker outfitted with helicopters to help find a way through the ice. Our expedition included visits to emperor penguins in the Ross Sea, helicopter flights to the ancient polar deserts known as the dry valleys, and the opportunity to pay our respects to Sir Ernest Shackleton's hut at Cape Royds, from where he so nearly reached the South Pole. Most moving of all was our pilgrimage to Sir Falcon Scott's Terra Nova hut at Cape Evans on Ross Island. Scott and his four companions set out for the South Pole on the 24 October 1911, never to return. By the time we arrived at New Zealand's subantarctic Campbell Islands we were filled with a sense of elation at having travelled to one of the most remote and barely habitable regions on earth, overwhelmed by its indescribable beauty. One last landing before Christchurch and the journey would come to an end.

Our Expedition Leader was a rather gruff but highly competent Canadian mariner. Shane was built like a grizzly bear with a beard to match. It had been a long trip, complicated by an outbreak of the dreaded norovirus or cruise ship virus, a highly contagious dysentery that spreads like wildfire. Vomiting, diarrhoea, stomach cramps and a mild fever can dull the enthusiasm of the most hardened traveller, and managing the guests' expectations had proved quite a challenge for Shane and the expedition crew. When we found the pack ice barring our way to the American base at McMurdo, some of the guests became very grumpy indeed. But all had been forgiven and forgotten by the time Campbell Island came into view, and we were excited at the thought of photographing the handful of royal albatrosses that breed here during the summer months.

As we stepped ashore Shane reminded us to be particularly careful about the Hooker's sea lions, also known as New Zealand sea lions, and to give them a wide berth. Angie and I nevertheless set off at a gallop, anxious to spend as much time with the albatrosses as we could. A long, winding, wooden stairway trailed off into the distance pointing us in the direction of the breeding colony. The vegetation reminded us of the stunted treescape from *Lord of the Rings*, straggly trees and bushes forming an interlocking tapestry of vegetation on either side of the boardwalk with a maze of tunnels and pathways where the sea lions sought access between the beaches and the higher ground.

I walked ahead of Angie, carrying a large rucksack full of camera gear on my back and a heavy tripod in one hand. Halfway along the trail a large male sea lion trundled into view, flip-flopping down the boardwalk. Shane's instructions had been to retreat in orderly fashion towards the ship if this happened. But having slogged this far up the path I was reluctant to head back. All we needed to do was to step off the walkway into the vegetation and the sea lion would surely continue on its way.

I told Angie to stay behind me, and stepped into the undergrowth. The sea lion, now moving rapidly towards us, decided that my way was his way. Did he envisage me as a rival perhaps? Was he attracted and antagonised by my movements? Or did he simply want to head for the beach along the same pathway he always used? Whatever was going through his mind it was evident that he now intended confronting me.

Animals tend to look even larger seen up close on foot. Given that the average male Hooker's sea lion weighs 320–450 kilograms and is 2.4–3.5 metres in length – twice the weight of a male African lion and longer – I had every reason to be concerned at my predicament. As the sea lion lumbered towards me with mouth agape revealing some very impressive teeth, I stepped backwards and instantly fell flat on my back in the bushes. I was thankful to be wearing a pair of heavy-duty insulated Antarctic rubber boots that along with my tripod I instinctively thrust towards the sea lion's open mouth, uttering every significant swear word I have ever wanted to string together in one previously unutterable sentence. The bull towered over me, looking every inch the heaving, huffing and puffing 'mountain-of-flesh-with-teeth' that is so intimidating to smaller rivals. Then, much to my relief, my venomous tirade, flailing rubber boots and club-like tripod did the trick and he turned and disappeared into the darkened world beneath the vegetation.

Shaken and barely able to rise from the ground with my heavy rucksack still strapped to my back, I staggered to my feet, double-checking that all my toes were still intact. I turned to look for Angie, expecting to be told what an idiot I was. But there was no sign of her. Then to my horror I heard yelling.

Angie had taken a tumble down the slope and was now desperately trying to scramble up and over shrubs and bushes pursued by a wave of moving vegetation that I knew could only be the sea lion. I galloped towards her, shouting and screaming at the top of my voice, desperately trying to reach her before the sea lion could bite her. At that moment she fell again with the sea lion barely a metre away. It felt as if I was running over an obstacle course as stunted trees collapsed under my headlong charge down the slope, a hundred fibrous arms reaching out to snag and trip my every step. When I reached Angie there was a sense of utter relief as we realised that the sea lion had gone and the terror of the moment drained from our faces. Only later did we discover that Angie had damaged a disc in her lower back when she twisted and fell, an injury that persists to this day as a reminder of our lucky escape.

We hobbled back to the pathway and as we did so, for an awful moment, the vegetation below us began to ripple and swirl again as the sea lion came back to haunt us one last time, exhibiting the same dogged persistence that makes the males such formidable foes in their battle for supremacy against members of their own kind. Most of the passengers had no idea of what had taken place, except for one or two who asked us later what we had been doing down there – had we seen something particularly interesting to photograph? All I could think about was what kind of roasting I would have endured from Shane if I had been mauled; all those years of experience garnered while living in the wild would have counted for nothing. When I spoke to him later he smiled and said:

'Any seasoned mariner will tell you that you can get a nasty infection from contact with a Hooker – in fact the infection is often worse than the bite!'

Jonathan and Angela Scott are award-winning photographers who live in Kenya, with a permanent base at Governor's Camp in the Maasai Mara Game Reserve. They are the only couple to have won the prestigious Wildlife Photographer of the Year Award as individuals and  are passionate conservationists. Jonathan has presented numerous wildlife television programmes for the BBC and Animal Planet including *Big Cat Diary*, which remains one of the most popular wildlife series on television, along with *Big Bear Diary*, *Elephant Diaries*, *The Secret Leopards* and *The Truth About Lions*. They travelled the world presenting wildlife stories for the American television series *Wild Things* in the late 1990s. Their book, *The Leopard's Tale*, was published recently by Bradt.

US versus the Broad
Oppressed Masses

Hilary Bradt

Irresponsible? Yes, of course it was, foolhardy to say the least. But, after nearly eleven months of Africa travels, we were just plain tired and our guard was down.

I can recall the scene so vividly: the bone-chilling cold of the foggy night air, the dark restaurant lit only by kerosene lanterns, and the intent brown faces of the students as they questioned us, the whites of their eyes the only clear part of their features. They all started the same way: 'My teacher says...'

If our bus hadn't broken down, George and I would have been in our little tent in Ethiopia's Bale Mountains, not whiling away the evening over a bottle of beer before going to our chilly room across the courtyard. Our bus had been sickly even before we started, needing a push from the passengers to encourage it to move, and as we gained altitude and the warm afternoon gave way to cool evening, it wheezed and coughed its way up the foothills before drawing to a groaning halt in a small town. The driver gestured to a hotel and we resigned ourselves to an unscheduled night in a typical country inn.

Cell-like rooms formed the three borders of the courtyard, the blue paint peeling on their doors, and a stinking toilet proclaimed its presence. The restaurant occupied the fourth side. We ate *injera* and *wat*, washing our hands in the chipped sink before tearing off chunks of foam-rubber-like flatbread to form a scoop for the sludgy stew or wat. We ordered a bottle of Castel between us and peered at the map in the gloaming, trying to work out where we were. It was too dark to write our diaries. Then half a dozen students joined us. The usual question: 'Where are you from?' 'England' I said, pointing to myself, and 'America' indicating George.

'My teacher says that black Americans aren't allowed to eat in a restaurant.'

'Oh no, that's not true. They changed that in the 1960s. Now they can eat wherever they want.'

'My teacher says that black Americans can't go to college!'

'That's not true either. In fact there's something called "affirmative action" which means that a black person is given priority. It makes up for all those years of discrimination. Honestly, it's so much better these days.'

More students arrived.

'But what about the Broad Oppressed Masses?'

That was when something snapped. We had just spent a week in Addis Ababa house-sitting for expat friends and listened each evening to the television news in English. It was shortly after the deposing of Haile Selassie, and every other phrase was about the Broad Oppressed Masses, and how they were rising up against their exploiters and the colonial enemies of Africa. We were always uncomfortably aware that we came into this category; America was not known for its communist sympathies. Kids threw stones at us in the street, and at one point while waiting for our bus to depart they finger-wrote CIA in the dirt on the window. Another time they surrounded us as we waited for a bus, chanting 'CIA, CIA'. And until that conversation we had held our peace, smiling sweetly and saying nothing.

'Actually,' I said, 'Poor people in New York have televisions.' The students were impressed. 'Yes, and very often they will have a car.' I was getting carried away, but I couldn't stop. 'Capitalism isn't all bad, you know. In America when people can't work the government gives them money. And if they are ill, and are poor or old, they get free medical care.'

These were outrageous statements (though broadly true) in a country as passionately Marxist as Ethiopia in 1976 and, believe me, if we had been in a capitalist country we would have taken the opposite stance. There were plenty more questions after that, and we rather warmed to the theme. It felt awfully good to talk freely after all those months of buttoned lips and caution.

A lone man was drinking at a neighbouring table. We were vaguely aware of his presence and the fact that he was listening to our conversation. Fine – it was time that Ethiopians learned another side of politics. The bartender collected the empty bottles and the students drifted away to their rooms. When the last one had gone our neighbour came over and introduced himself. 'I'm an army lieutenant.' He waited for the implication to sink in. 'You have been praising capitalism. That is against the law and you are under arrest. I shall come for you at six o'clock tomorrow morning and take you to the District Officer. What room are you in?' Then he left.

George and I looked at each other in sheer terror. I stood up but my legs were trembling so much that I had to sit down again. We had good reason to be afraid. Although we had only been in Ethiopia a week or so we had had plenty of time to learn that the government was utterly ruthless in wiping out its enemies, and that any foreigner from a capitalist country was under suspicion. A few days earlier we had met a Canadian working for a famine relief programme. He smiled wryly when we told him how shocked we were to see sacks of grain in the market with the stamp 'A gift from the American people'. 'It's good that it was for sale; sometimes they just throw it away. They claim that the grain is poisoned.' He went on to tell us how he and his driver had been stopped in the desert by a group of vigilantes who accused him of being a spy. His driver acted as interpreter. 'They say take your shoes off,' he said. Mike complied. 'Now follow them.'

'Well, you know those harpoon thorns that you get in the desert. Huge prickles. I was hobbling along trying to avoid the worst of them. After a while I asked my driver where they were taking me. He had a conversation with them and said: "They say they're going to shoot you".' I can't remember how Mike avoided that fate, but the story was still vividly in our minds. We both knew what could happen if things went badly the following day.

We didn't sleep well. For one thing it was freezing cold and we had only one blanket, but even under the softest goose down we wouldn't have slept. What would happen to us? How could we be so stupid as to have that sort of conversation? Heavens, it wasn't even the sort of thing we'd normally say! During our wakeful night we considered our options. Try to flee before we were called for? No, without transport and hopelessly conspicuous with our heavy backpacks, we'd soon be picked up. And anyway, we hadn't committed a crime – not in our eyes, anyway. We had to stay the course.

Our lieutenant was as good as his word. At six he was there, in uniform this time, with an army truck. This wasn't the first time we'd been arrested in Africa and we'd learned a few survival techniques. We brought our passports, and plenty of reading matter. Fear is bad enough but combined with boredom it can be toxic. Our last arrest had seen us incarcerated on a disabled vehicle at Kampala bus station after a misguided attempt to go to a botanical garden in a town called Entebbe. Bad timing. The 'Entebbe Raid' had taken place a couple of days before, so in hindsight we couldn't really blame the jittery army for assuming we were spies. We had one book between us, so George read a page, tore it out, and passed it to me. We sat in that bus for three hours, reading Alberto Moravia under the watchful eye of a kid with a machine gun, before being released. Not to freedom, the army chap made it clear, but to turn ourselves in at the police station. His superior officer had run out of petrol and couldn't come to interrogate us.

That time we had no intention of obeying orders. We fled to our hotel, packed our rucksacks, and took the first train to Nairobi, our hearts fluttering as we crossed the border into Kenya. It was only there, in the British Council Reading Room, that we realised just how serious the situation had been. 'Get them out alive!' screamed the headline of the *Daily Mail*. 'Them' were the British nationals remaining in Uganda.

Now, in this remote region of Ethiopia, we were led into a smart office. The District Officer rose to his feet, resplendent in beautifully pressed khaki, knife-edge creases to his trousers, polished black shoes. His skin was the colour of milk chocolate, his features aquiline, and his accent Sandhurst. We shook hands and I noticed the long, graceful fingers with manicured nails.

'Now what is this all about?'

Haltingly we launched into our prepared speech. How we loved and admired Ethiopia, how impressed we were with what the country had achieved, how beautiful was the landscape, how rich the culture, and how fascinating the wildlife. 'We've heard that there are Simien wolves in the Bale Mountains. We were planning to spend a few days looking for them.' Our lieutenant popped the top of his biro up and down, his eyes lowered. 'They were talking about politics. They must learn not to do that.' The officer raised his eyebrows. 'We should teach them a lesson. Like those Australians last week.'

'Oh my dear fellow, I don't think we need to go to those extremes.'

He looked at us for a few moments without speaking. Surely my trembling was visible? 'The situation in the mountains is... not easy. If you go there you would be at risk. I am giving you twenty-four hours to leave Ethiopia. You understand?' We nodded, shook hands and left.

I recall no sense of relief as our unsmiling lieutenant drove us back to the hotel. That came later as we discussed whether we should obey orders and leave Ethiopia. We decided to risk staying – our speech to the officer had been true. We did love the country and wanted to see more. But it was not hard to abandon our plans to look for wolves in those mountains.

A few days later we heard on television that 'twenty-eight enemies of the masses have been liquidated in Bale'.

That lieutenant and our sickly bus had, perhaps, saved our lives.

Hilary Bradt's visit to Ethiopia was part of an eleven-month journey through Africa which resulted in the second Bradt guide, *Backpacker's Africa*. This book helped launch the publishing company which is now celebrating its fortieth anniversary. She returned to Ethiopia in 2010 on a newspaper commission to write about the changes that had taken place and found the country transformed. Hilary received an MBE for Services to the Travel Industry in 2008 and a Lifetime Achievement Award from the British Guild of Travel Writers in 2009.

Walking the Border
Jonathan Lorie

'A re you sure they can kill you?' I crouched in the wet ditch, hoping they wouldn't see me in the dark. Somewhere under the trees, blurry shapes were stirring.

'Oh yes,' whispered Adam, 'with their hooves or with their horns. Can you make less noise?'

I stopped scratching at a tin of ravioli with the Swiss Army penknife that was all we had for cooking equipment, and pondered the wetness of my jeans. How long would it be till we could get some sleep or dry clothes? Then the moon came out and floodlit our position.

The oak woods and rushing streams around Offa's Dyke on the borders of Wales are beautiful by moonlight. But not when you're spooked at 2 a.m. by the ravings of your walking companion, on the first adventure of your life at the bold age of fifteen.

Two nights into our hike – planned as a week-long jaunt of camping rough, roaming wild and writing nature poetry – and I was beginning to have my doubts.

It was Adam who had suggested the trip, one airless afternoon in the dog days of the summer term – those drifting days when suddenly your school desk is too small and your blazer feels too tight and the blue sky beyond the classroom windows is a torment as well as a promise. He'd punched my arm as the ex-Shakespearean actor who was our English master swept out of the room, trailing clouds of mothballs. 'Guess what I'm doing this summer?'

I slammed shut my copy of Wordsworth's longer poems and sighed. 'Retaking your exams?'

'No way,' he grinned, tugging a folded map from his blazer pocket. It burst out with a shower of pencil shavings and paper clips and toffee wrappers. 'I'm off to the wilds of Wales. Offa's Dyke, ancient wall against the Celts, site of Dark Age battles, inspiration to Mr Wordsworth... And more importantly, 160 miles of remote countryside without a teacher or parent in sight. You wanna come?'

Perhaps that's how adventures always begin: with a glint in the eye and no clue of what's involved. With a wish to cross a border. I said yes at once, and the last week of term flashed by in a frenzy of rucksacks, grid references and warnings from my dad. His army training was finally coming in handy. 'Never use up your reserves,' he said, handing me a tenner. 'Always camp before nightfall. And look out for snakes.'

He drove us there, at the end of July. It was a long day's drive in the puttering Volkswagen camper that had inspired my childhood sense of adventure. Sixty miles an hour was probably all it did. We had camped wild in it across Cornwall and Brittany, as you could in the 1970s, with nothing between us and the forces of nature except a paraffin lamp and a strange folding spade that Dad had picked up in World War Two and thought was as good as a toilet.

Adam and I were dropped off, like two commandos on a raid, by the ruins of Tintern Abbey. The Dyke began just above. I recall the grin on my younger brother's face as the van chugged away. He knew he was headed for a hotel in Cardiff.

Adam had already alarmed them, at a hostelry somewhere on the road, when we ordered lunch. Mine was chicken in the basket, a speciality of the period. His was a nut roast. My father eyed him suspiciously.

And so the walk began. The ruined walls of the abbey filled the valley below us as we trekked into a copse of hazels edged with bracken. We'd read about this place at school – its 'steep woods and lofty cliffs', as Wordsworth once described them. His ecstatic poem on Tintern Abbey had set alight the Romantic age and our romantic youth. Often we'd read his work aloud to one another, in a deserted classroom in an empty lunch hour. His writing pulsed with a sense that something bigger than our everyday lives could be found in places like this – in 'the wild green landscape' and 'the light of setting suns'. And here we were to find it.

Or so we said to each other, as the sun vanished faster than my family and left us blundering through the darkness in a wood without a plan. We had a map, but it didn't seem to correspond with the hills and trees on the ground. 'If we stick to the path,' said Adam, tripping over a tree root, 'we can't go wrong.'

Eventually the lights of a stone farmhouse loomed out of the trees. We knocked on its door. A dog exploded into snarls and barks, possibly on the other side. But no-one came.

We wandered on. In a river meadow by a boggy stream we pitched our two-man tent, Adam laying out the pegs and me banging them in with a shoe. He'd forgotten the mallet. We'd both forgotten to bring food. We crawled inside, hungry, tired and elated, and fell asleep within minutes.

The morning dawned pink and fresh. Which is more than could be said for us, drenched in last night's sweat and aching for a meal. I poked my head out of the tent flap. 'Looks like Wales to me.'

A thin drizzle misted our steps as we rolled up the canvas and stalked on to the path. Strictly speaking, Offa's Dyke is a bank of earth fronted by a defensive ditch, running hundreds of miles along what is still the border between England and Wales. But in rainy weather it's a heap of mud sliding into a channel of slime, along a purgatory we'd chosen for ourselves. And I was wearing desert boots.

After an hour, the path sloped down to a village. Luckily its single shop was open. The bell trilled merrily as we pushed open the net-curtained door.

'Hello my ducks, what will you have?' asked a grey-haired woman behind the counter. We looked around us, dazed. There was food everywhere.

Shakily we piled boxes of groceries on to the counter. She rang it all up, and then we tried to fit it into our rucksacks. Boxes of cereal, tea and sugar, sausages for me, carrots for him, a glass jar of pickled onions for both of us, plus Marmite, gobstoppers, a squishy pat of butter, two loaves of Mother's Pride – they all went down the hole somehow, snuggled next to hiking socks and sleeping bags, nicely melding together. We staggered out, burdened but happy, promising ourselves a good square meal in the woods above.

'Ah,' said Adam, as we stopped for lunch. 'I forgot the matches. And actually the paraffin for the stove. D'you think it matters?'

I looked at him and looked away. The rain had stopped and the view was superb. The Dyke ran off across sweeping hills with lush green fields on either side, dotted with ancient oaks. 'Probably not. We could have that tin of pilchards on bread.'

'Ah,' he grinned, 'I forgot the tin opener too.'

I handed him my penknife as a penance, and while he gouged open a can I read aloud from *A Shropshire Lad*, a mournful collection of ballads about the borderlands. This was what we'd come for, I thought, tucking into a mouthful of fish oil – life in the raw.

We started off again. The footpath stretched through fields of sheep and slender copses, then up on to rolling fields. Sometimes it was lined with boulders or bracken, drystone walls or rickety fences. From these great hills, we could see for miles.

All afternoon we walked. We passed no-one. We ran out of things to say. We ate all the chocolate. We drank all the water. My soggy boots did not dry out.

On a particularly testing slope, I realised that I'd never actually hiked before – not for more than an hour on the South Downs. Every footstep felt like lead. Home seemed far away.

'The Black Hills are over there,' said Adam, by way of encouragement, gesturing at a distant horizon. The name did not help. I had visions of spoil heaps, mountains of shale and slag, blackened wastelands where we trudged forever through dust. 'We'll probably reach them,' he mused, 'in two more days.'

That night we made camp a little earlier. A farmer let us pitch in his field. 'Now don't disturb the herd,' he warned. We didn't care. I eased off my boots and splashed in a stream to soothe the blisters. Adam rattled around with plates and tins and the penknife. I picked up a book but couldn't be bothered to read any more.

After a supper of cold spaghetti hoops, we stretched out in the tent and talked about the lives we hoped we'd have, our hopes and fears and friends and dreams. Night fell and we droned on, rolled in our sleeping bags, warm against the darkness. Maybe this wouldn't be so bad. Then Adam heard a thud outside that froze him in mid-flow.

'It's cows,' he hissed.

'And?'

'They can kill you with one blow of their hooves.'

'Don't be bloody silly.'

'No, it's true. They can't see the tent in the dark, and then they walk straight over your face as you lie there asleep – and their weight can cave in a human head just like a teaspoon through an eggshell.'

He was sitting bolt upright, a tremble in his voice.

I'd no idea. Back home I'd spent whole summers camping in the garden in Sussex with my friends, but that didn't include live cows. It did include ghost stories that scared us half to death. One night there'd been a storm that nearly took the tent and we'd all run back to my house in fear.

I could hear Adam scrabbling into clothes. Cursing softly, I hauled on my jeans and scrambled across the tent. I stubbed my foot on a tin and angrily shoved it into the pocket of my cagoule. Out in the field, huge shadows were shifting beneath the oaks. We scuttled across some nettles and lurched into a ditch. It was full of water. Up to our knees. Of course we had no torch.

'Is it a bull?' I whispered.

'Doesn't matter,' he muttered, 'they're all as deadly in the dark.'

We crouched and watched. Nothing happened. Water trickled somewhere. The air felt cool. So did my soaking trousers.

'Wordsworth didn't have this problem,' I whispered. But Adam didn't smile. I pulled out the tin and penknife from my pocket. Even uncooked ravioli might cheer things up. Adam stopped me.

After half an hour of crouching in ditch water peering at shadows, I'd had enough. 'Can we go back?' I murmured, but he was still transfixed. 'Alright,' I announced, in a voice loud enough to scare off any bull, 'I'm going back to the tent.'

I marched across the field. A scattering of cows lumbered away. My sleeping bag had never felt so warm.

Next morning was not easy. There was no hot water for tea and no conversation between us. I pulled on my damp jeans slowly. This was not what we had planned. Another five days of this? I knew what I wanted to do.

'Adam,' I said with all the finesse of a fifteen-year-old, 'I'm going home.'

He stared at me.

'We haven't eaten or slept comfortably for two days. My feet are killing me. I'm cold and I'm bored. Give me the map.'

'But it's my summer holiday.'

'I'm really, really sorry. Now pass the map.'

My exit was swift enough. I found the nearest road and flagged down a country bus. Its speed was fantastic – and it had seats. It stopped in the medieval streets of Monmouth town, but I had no time for history now. I jumped aboard a National Express and headed straight for home.

The next thing I remember is stepping off at our bus station in the gentle folds of Sussex, and phoning our house. Mum's voice answered: 'Hello love, how's the walk?'

I took a gulp of air. 'Can you come and fetch me?'

She sounded a little surprised. 'Where from, dear, in Wales?'

'No Mum,' I said slowly, 'Horsham station.'

They picked me up by car, my brother smirking on the back seat. Our house seemed bigger and warmer than when I left. There was a log fire in the living room. My grey Siamese hopped on to my lap. Then my brother slowly asked, 'So what went wrong?'

It's funny how you never escape from your very first adventures. They set the course. For thirty-five years I've followed and fled the echoes of this trip. I've become a traveller by trade and a writer at last. I've camped in worse places, caught more trouble and survived on worse meals than I did then. But sometimes I'm still a kid in a field of shadows, wondering how I got here and how far it is to home. And my family still like to remind me, when they hear news of any failure of mine. 'Oh yes,' they nod to each other, 'but don't you remember Offa's Dyke?'

Jonathan Lorie is a travel writer and former editor of *Traveller* magazine. He teaches travel writing through his agency, Travellers' Tales, and takes his children to Wales every spring.

Road Trip
Alex Robinson

This is what it's like to be chased. I skid around another bend, my lights panning over the chicane and out to distant rainforest on the far side of the valley. The wheels squeal. The rain is falling in sheets now. And they're still behind me, right on my tail, their black pick-up weaving and bobbing in the rear-view mirror, desperate to overtake and block the road again.

I floor the accelerator and the tiny Fiat engine revs so hard it sounds like its pistons will burst, the road lines flashes of light in the glistening black. The car claws back a precious few metres from my pursuers. Then they speed up, swerve to the left and are level with me. Their window's down. The driver's shouting across the narrow gap, his face explosive with rage. '*Para o carro filho da puta!*' Stop the car! But I've accelerated just enough. I'm into the next bend. They brake hard and are behind me once again.

It's got to be soon. Paraty's got to be soon!

But there's still no sign of the town. No lights through the rain. No life. No headlights approaching the other way. No... wait. What's that? There's a shimmer through the trees, just round the next bend. I floor the accelerator again and leap into the corner, the car lurching towards the precipice at the edge of the road before swinging violently back into another straight. I see a single light – four hundred metres away. A house? Three hundred... There's a sign, 'Mecânico', dripping with rain. Two hundred... Yes! A house. That means people. One hundred... I swing in and pull to a halt, horn blaring.

Someone's bound to emerge. The pick-up will whizz past.

It doesn't. And the house stays quiet. I'm caught. The pick-up pulls in behind me, headlamps blazing. They get out. Big black pistols in their hands, right index fingers on the triggers. Left index fingers across their lips.

The older one's at my passenger window now, gun pointing through the glass.

'*Abre a porta*!' he mouths. Open the door. The house is still silent. Is there really no-one there? Or are they looking out, terrified, through darkened windows? The gunman gets into my car. He's in the passenger seat now. The barrel is pressed against my temple. This is it.

'You've caused enough trouble,' he says, his face all pits and shadows in the patchy reflected light of the pick-up's headlamps. His eyes are as black and hard as a shark's. How could I have been so foolish? How could I have thought he was friendly? He points back to the dark, and the road. 'Drive.' And I drive into the night, beams cutting into the rain, his friend following behind in the black pick-up.

If only I'd left earlier that morning. As usual I'd put things off until the last moment, waking a little too late to a bright São Paulo day, taking a little too long over breakfast. The morning seemed perfect now. I savour every detail. Thick coffee. What a great flavour coffee has. I can almost taste it. Such a perfect morning. The three of us at breakfast. Sun streaming through the windows, the early morning light as warm and thick as melting butter. The smell of crispy Brazilian bread, fresh from the bakery on the corner. Orange juice in the glasses. Gardenia and Raphael so beautiful, light playing in their hair. They were planning a day in the park. The sunlight bringing out the colours in their eyes. Raphael clapping his hands together in front of Mummy. Big grin. Chocolate spread all over his face.

I didn't want to drive to the coast. Five long hours in a hot car on my own for a single lousy commission that would barely pay for the petrol. I threw some things in a case. Gathered the lenses and cameras together. Computer.

Mobile. Raincoat just in case. Driver's licence, ID, CPF, insurance, tax details. Bloody Brazilian bureaucracy… Did I really have to go? I guess so. It was for a broadsheet. My first. More commissions would surely come. I grabbed my bags. The keys.

Then the phone call came. Gardenia picked it up as I was halfway out the door. It was Chico, her brother.

'Send him my love,' I said on my way out.

But hang on. What was he saying? A bomb? In London?!

I came back inside. Dumped my bags, rushed to the TV. A wrecked bus near Baker Street… Tatters of clothes… Were they clothes? People with blood caked on their faces. Tony Blair speaking at a hasty press conference lit by strobe-light flashes. A bottle-blonde Globo reporter at the scene. '*Ataque terrorista… Londrinos num estado de choque…*'

I spent hours on the phone checking with everyone I could think of. Thank God. They were all safe. Thank God.

It was nearly lunchtime before I reached for the car keys again and headed for the highway, mind buzzing with London. Avenida 23 de Maio was crawling with cars. What did I expect? My mind drifted as the jam cleared. Bombs. Violence. It all seemed so immediate, and yet so strangely far away from São Paulo. I passed giant air-brushed and super-colour saturated hoardings pinned to the skyscrapers – a chef in white holding a skewer of fatty meat, Ivete Sangalo with pearly white teeth and tiny shorts beckoning with a can of ice-cold beer – *super gelada*! Then an evangelical church the size of a warehouse, a gutter-like canal filled with rubbish. It was so far from London. My thoughts drifting, I missed my turn. Then I got lost on the Minhocão, the snaking multi-lane raised highway that winds through the stacked concrete in the city's west like a giant graphite-grey worm wiggling through egg boxes. There's no way off for kilometres. Eventually I doubled back through hilly streets lined with jacarandas. Vast gated homes. Ramshackle breeze-block dwellings. Underpasses strewn with graffiti. Finally I was back on to Avenida

23 de Maio. But it was past three before the clutter of favelas on São Paulo's edge were behind me, before the stench of the river had given way to the spicy sweetness of the forest.

The sky became vast, the space almost infinite. I was a speck in the continental vastness of Brazil. The motorway hours passed in toll stations and processions of thundering trucks. When I reached the turn-off for Taubaté and the coast road the sun was low in the sky. And I was bursting for a piss.

There were no services for tens of kilometres. Bollocks! I'd have to hold it in – the Taubaté road was notorious for bandits. It narrowed into a single lane highway and began to wind and turn, banking to the right, climbing towards the Serra do Mar mountains. I passed ramshackle homesteads, doors closed now in the late afternoon. Signs scrawled outside offered 'cachaça artesanal' – moonshine, and freshly picked *caju* fruit. Behind them steep hillsides of scrubby grass dotted with termite mounds and speckled with cattle rose towards dark green forest. Not far now to a service station, and not far from there to Paraty.

But I had to go. It was a Thursday; the bandits would be off duty, still resting from the last weekend's rich pickings. I'd be OK. I pulled to a stop on an embankment next to a grove of eucalyptus, and rushed out of the car. The door bounced back on its spring, swung shut behind me. And locked. With the keys in the ignition.

My phone was inside. What could I do? Try as I might I couldn't prize the windows down. Nor could I bring myself to smash the glass. I picked up a rock and struck the glass gingerly, but didn't have the guts to break it. So I flagged down help. This was a busy road. No-one was going to rob me here and risk being seen. Car after car whizzed past. Then a big black pick-up stopped next to me. Two men got out: one in his fifties, thin and wiry, dark hair thinning on top, jeans and a worn t-shirt; the other younger, round-faced, smiling. They looked like country folk – maybe a father and son. The older man greeted me with effortless Brazilian affability. Nice guys.

'*O que aconteceu?*' What happened? '*Onde vai?*' Where you going?

He laughed when I told him I'd locked myself out of the car, slapped me on the back. He'd done the same once. Embarrassment evaporated. These were good guys. Not bandits. I was OK. The older man started tugging on the lock, pushing down on the windows. Did he know what he was doing? Yeah. He'd had a Fiat once too. He chatted casually as he worked, pushing down at the window through the rubber seal, harder than I would have dared. A tiny gap appeared at the top.

'You're not Brazilian?'

'No. British.'

'You speak Portuguese well.'

All Brazilians say that. But it made me feel good. He asked me where I was going. Paraty, I said, to interview a writer. I didn't mention the cameras.

'And this music, what is it?' The stereo was booming inside the locked car.

'Rock,' I said. 'Led Zeppelin.'

'Oh, Ledgy Zeplinny, Hobertch Planchee. Great singer. You like it, Guto?'

The fat guy grinned. He loved it too. I was OK. These were great, regular guys. They'd get into the car. I'd give them the CD when they did.

But the window wasn't budging any more.

Maybe we could pull up the lock through the gap? I suggested.

Great idea. Why hadn't they thought of that?

'Go and get some pliers from the truck, Guto,' said the older man.

Guto returned and handed them over. The older man used them to cut the car aerial, bending it into a loop and shoving it down through the gap in the window. After a few attempts the lock popped up. Smiling, back-slapping.

'*Obrigado, amigo.*' Thanks, mate. I gave them the CD. They thanked me, and got back in their car.

'*Ciao, amigo.* Be careful on this road, my friend. You never know who you'll meet.' And they sped off.

I felt light, relieved. An hour later I'd reached the coast, navigated the one-way system in Ubatuba town and was on the last stretch of road before Paraty.

It was night by now and had begun to rain. Ubatuba's last houses thinned behind me and the road plunged into darkness. I didn't see another car for kilometres, just the occasional dirt track. Soon each side of the highway was thick with bromeliad-encrusted trees. A coatimundi ran across the road far ahead, cutting through the headlights. Maybe I'd see an ocelot?

The trees thinned occasionally to the right. By day these gaps would have shown a sweep of pristine rainforest and long, deserted tropical beaches washed by a bottle-green Atlantic. Now there was just blackness.

The car began to climb. The last mountain spur, I thought. Thirty kilometres to go. Nearly there. Thank God.

Then a big black pick-up overtook me. The same black pick-up. And the lights were off. I'd told them I was going to Paraty. And they knew there was only one way there – on a road which would be deserted at this time of night. No witnesses for a robbery.

When I came round the next bend, they'd blocked the road – parked right across it. I accelerated and swerved round the truck, barely a metre to spare. And that's how the chase had begun.

Now the older man is sitting next to me. The affability he showed earlier has changed into cold hunger. The gun is on his lap: icy, metallic brutality. I'd seen its eye, looked down its dark iris into nothingness. The man's eyes were as black. Empty. Why had I told this bastard where I was going? Why hadn't I smashed my own car window? Why did I stop at the mechanic's house? Why? Why?

'Turn left here,' he says, pistol-whipping me in the leg. Frozen into numbness, I turn into a dirt road cutting through the forest. The rainwater streams down in rivulets, flowing into gullies. Trees tower above us. The big black pick-up bobs and veers in the rear-view mirror. But I don't notice the bumps. I'm like a rodent caught by a cat. Passive. Incredulous. We drive for about two kilometres, up into the hills. Then he tells me to stop and get out of the car.

'Watch him,' he tells Guto, who is as nervous as I am. Guto bumbles, puts his gun in his trousers and stares at me. 'No! Point the gun at him, you fat idiot!'

Guto mumbles an apology, approaches. He looks awkward with the gun. There's alcohol on his breath, and cocaine in his bloodshot, wide eyes.

The older man is as calm as a contract killer. He opens my car boot.

'What do we have here? Cameras, computer, very nice. You didn't tell us about these did you?' He puts them in the pick-up and comes back to my car.

'And in the glove compartment? Any *maconha*? You middle-class kids always have weed ready for the beach don't you? Your phone. Piece of shit. I don't want that. Or the CDs.'

'You can have it all,' I tell him.

… All my cameras, I think, my database of pictures…

'Of course we can. You think you can stop us?'

I don't react. Soon he's emptied the car. Then he empties my pockets, wallet, ID cards, all gone. But he doesn't want the car and hurls the keys contemptuously into the forest.

Then he turns to his friend. Guto's gun is still pointing at my head and he says slowly and nonchalantly, 'OK Guto. Kill him. We'll burn his car.'

In that moment something shifts deep inside, behind the mind, deeper even than my emotions. They fade, disappear, and in a second I sense everything. The rain slows until it falls like plankton drifting through the current in deep sea. It gathers on a leaf, pools and gently drips off. Even in the dark the greens are so intense they almost seem illuminated, and my nose fills with the scent of the forest, the sharp spiciness of the razor grass, the dampness of mycelia and epiphytes, the rich, oxygen-filled air. A thousand images and impressions flood into my mind. Childhood, school, my parents, home in Sussex, Bristol, Cambridge, India, Gardenia in Hackney. And at home. I see a tiny Huichol Mexican woman standing strong between two angry Scandinavian drunks in a bar in Tulum. Staring deeply into each of their eyes in turn, breathing from the belly, pulling the rage from each of them. I see Ashishda in his room in Mirtola high in the Indian Himalayas, holding out a coin. 'Can you see it?' He asks. 'Can you see that you see it? What happens to the seeing when I take it away?' And then I see Raphael in his chair at breakfast, chocolate all round his mouth. And I have clarity.

I am here. Now.

And I look the older man straight in the eye. Deeply, down into the depths of that darkness, into him.

'Do you want my three-year-old boy to be left without a daddy?' I ask. 'Take it. All my stuff. I don't know who you are or why you are here. I don't care. You can have it all.'

He stares back at me. And suddenly he sees me and is a man, a sad, desperate man. He pauses. Guto pauses. It's all happened in a moment.

'Where did you meet us?'

'I don't remember.'

'What kind of car do we have?'

'I don't know.'

'I know everyone in Paraty. If you tell the police, I'll find you.'

He has my ID document. My address.

'I'll kill you and your family.'

Then he looks up to the sky.

'*Deus me olha!*' he cries. 'I am letting this gringo go free. Be my witness. Walk up the road, gringo. Don't look back. Don't come back for half an hour.'

I set off.

'Gringo!' he calls me back. 'Take your coat,' handing me my jacket. 'It's raining.'

Up the dirt track. Up the dirt track. Forest all around me. Forest. Up the dirt track. Walk. Don't look back.

I'm over the brow of a tiny hill. They can't see me.

I fall out of my trance. I'm in the middle of the road! What the hell am I doing? I run into the trees, twenty, thirty, forty metres into the dark. Into the thick forest.

Just in time. The pick-up roars up the road. Halts just thirty metres from me. But I am lost in the dark. The trees are all around me.

'*Esta onde, o filho da puta*? Where is the bastard?' the older man shouts above the noise of the engine and the roar of the rain.

'I'm here,' I think. And I am free. And there is only life, awareness and bliss.

Alex Robinson is based in London. He travels extensively in Latin America and South East Asia writing and photographing for publications including *Sunday Times Travel*, the *New York Times*, *The Guardian* and *Vanity Fair*. He is a multi-award winner – with a National Magazine award in the US and a Premio Abril de Jornalismo in Brazil among others. He is the author of guidebooks to Brazil, including Bradt's *Bahia: The Heart of Brazil's Northeast*.

A Pestle and Mortar
in Paradise

Ella Pawlik

I returned from the Lost City. I nearly didn't.

It was the rainy season in Colombia, and the torrents of water that poured down the mountainside were washing the road away. Our jeep ascent into the Sierra Nevada involved driving with one wheel overlapping the edge of a sheer precipice. We had two contraguerrilla guards accompanying us in the truck and the butt of one of their rifles tapped politely on my hip bone.

Climbing out of the jeep at the top, we met a group that had just finished their trek to La Ciudad Perdida. They looked haggard and we asked them how it had gone. One man thought long and hard, and replied: 'It's like meeting with the devil.' And so we set off. Uphill and sweaty – we were floundering mounds of uselessness. Our guides didn't seem to notice. We finally made it to the top and spent the first night sleeping in hammocks under the stars.

We rose with the sun and saw paradise. The butterflies were incandescent and bigger than birds. The bromeliad-lined trees were colossal, and there were flowers so fleshy they looked like fruit. I fell in love with the world all over again. And again. And again. And I didn't stop until we stopped walking. On the second night we camped right next to the ferocious Buritaca River. Slowly but surely we were working our way into the obscurity of jungle. Mosquitoes and sandflies became squadrons of bloodsucker fuckers.

The next day we began the final stretch to the Lost City. On the way, we swam in a crystal pool with waterfalls, and I submerged myself fully in the glorious moment. Then we had to cross that river, the ferocious one. Seven times. The current was so strong we used ropes to get from one side to the other, and we bobbed around like cumbersome blubber balls while our guides balanced expertly on nothing. Safely on the right side, we soggily approached the stone steps to the Lost City, and climbed all 2,000 of them.

There. It was beautiful. Crumbling stone circle terraces rose implausibly out of the mountains like rejected offerings to the clouds. Serene. Detached. A whole land, a whole civilisation built on the dreams of dawn. And the jungle had reclaimed everything. Rising with the sun again on the fourth day, we toured the ancient city with our guide. Three snakes and a toucan later, we began the long trek home.

It turns out the devil was in a tree root. Forgetting the importance of looking down as well as up when trekking, I tripped over it, and fell on to the rocks below. Lying with my face in the mud, and my knee and the rock like a pestle and mortar, all I could think of was the word 'splat'. I briefly saw my pristine white kneecap, and then the blood started. With no option but to continue, I dragged my leg behind me, also trying to ignore the stabbing pain in my side. At base our guide boiled some water and salt to try and clean the hole in my knee, although he forgot to cool it first. I couldn't cover my leg up so the mosquitoes and sandflies feasted on it. At one point, a moth got stuck in the wound.

I had to conquer some deeply unforgiving inclines the next day. By the time we reached base for our last night my leg was so swollen it was starting to blend in with the ancient jungle trees. Waiting for the jeep to come and collect us, I noticed the swelling had spread up one leg and was creeping down the other. Both my legs were shiny and purple and it was becoming hard to tell where the joints were. The precarious drive down didn't seem nearly as scary this time as I was concentrating on trying not to let my legs explode. We got back to Santa Marta in floods – there was no way of telling where the sea ended and the road began. A pathetic fallacy of grey.

In hospital, I was treated for a cracked rib and cellulitis. 'Just in time,' apparently. I had an antibiotic shot from a needle so wide it felt like a gutter, and was given millions of pills to lay my head on. For a week after, I dragged round swollen, fluid-filled legs, waiting patiently for the infection to subside.

It was worth it. I saw what should and shouldn't have been lost. I would do it all again. And, it would appear that I took the Satan bullet for the whole trekking group. Everyone else was completely fine.

Ella Pawlik lives in Bristol and is a freelance writer. When possible, she travels to Other Places and writes from there too. Ella's life is centred around music, people, the smell of earth and the sound of birds, and trying to describe how beautiful they all are. She also has to concentrate very hard on not falling over, with varying degrees of success. When it all goes wrong she turns mishaps into stories, gets shortlisted for the Bradt/*Independent on Sunday* Travel Writing Competition, and feels happy for silver linings.

Something to Declare
Mike Unwin

It's past midnight. My fellow passengers are sprawled in awkward abandon across the hard bench seats of the railway carriage – some folded over luggage, others squash-faced against windows. The pulse of communal snoring ebbs and flows above the rhythmic clatter of the rails. Our train rumbles on into the night, eating up the dark miles of thorn scrub that is southeastern Botswana after dark.

I'm not asleep though, and neither is Louise. Hardly surprising, what with the nodding cranium of our companion Dennis thudding into her left shoulder at every jolt of the rails. Upright, anxious, her eyes glint in the carriage's one weak overhead light. 'Now,' she hisses. 'Do it now.'

I get to my feet and, for the umpteenth time, scan up and down the carriage. Nobody appears to be watching. There's no sign of movement. The border guards are far behind us – even now staggering out of some shebeen, no doubt, or tucked up in bed, dreaming of sniffer dogs and smugglers.

The aisle is an obstacle course. I manoeuvre over outstretched legs and hefty baggage, steadying myself against the sway to avoid accidentally grabbing a sleeping face. A judder prompts one snorer to grunt and shift, stopping me dead. False alarm: the carriage remains insensible to my progress. Reaching the end, I pass into the interim corridor, stepping over a film-reel blur of tracks beneath the gap at my feet, and find myself standing between the closed doors of two toilets. Mine is the one to the left. I grasp the handle.

But wait. Suppose they're watching me. Suppose they know exactly what I've done and are lying in ambush. One more step and the night will explode into lights, yells, whistles and uniforms. They'll have me red-handed.

No, this is just paranoia. From here I can see the full length of two carriages and there isn't a sign of life. Besides, can't a man answer a call of nature? I ease down the window to let in a face-slap of cold air then, steeling myself to the task in hand, turn the handle and slip inside.

It's dark. The light fitting dangles bulb-less. But perhaps that's a blessing: my last visit to this cramped, fetid cubicle suggested that it didn't bear too close a scrutiny. Anyway, the moonlight is enough to work by. Lowering the toilet lid as noiselessly as I can without fingering too much of its unpleasant underside, I climb up on top.

There, high on the outer wall, is the hatch – closed, just as I'd left it three hours earlier. Behind the small, hinged door is a recess through which the guard inserts the train's destination sign, spelling it out for those on the platform. When our journey began, back at Bulawayo railway station, this sign had read Gaborone. There can surely have been no need to change it since then.

It's not the sign that I'm interested in, though. On a narrow shelf behind the door sits a fat wad of cash: pounds sterling, US dollars and Zimbabwe dollars. I know, because I put it there. And now I've come to take it back.

But there's a problem. The hatch is shut tight. I run my fingers around the frame, searching for a fingertip grip with which to prise it open. No joy. Now I can make out the small metal keyhole. Locked. But it hadn't been locked earlier. The catch must have engaged when I closed it. My heart sinks as I now recall a distinct click. I thump on the door. The thud resounds around the cubicle and, no doubt, down the corridor outside. I shrink from the noise. Clearly, brute force is not an option.

I should explain: I'm not a habitual smuggler of contraband. In fact, I like to think I'm not really a criminal at all. This incident took place in April 1989. I was newly arrived in Zimbabwe – just ten years independent back then, and widely celebrated as an African success story. To me, fresh out of university, the country seemed ripe with opportunity and adventure.

The trouble was, I needed a car. I'd laboured around the country by train, bus and hitchhiking, but without my own wheels its wildest corners had remained out of reach. And cars in 1989 Zimbabwe were gold dust. Trade restrictions with then-Apartheid South Africa meant no new vehicles, while any secondhand jalopy that went for sale, however decrepit, was snapped up pronto – and not by those, like me, on a government teacher's salary.

Botswana was the answer. Zimbabwe's neighbour had no tiresome ethical qualms about trading with the evil regime, and its garage forecourts were said to glitter with secondhand vehicles direct from Pretoria. Just nip across to Gaborone and you'd pick one up for peanuts. And, while there, why not stock up on tuna, rice, light bulbs and all those other imported goods denied the long-suffering residents of Bulawayo? Every entrepreneurial Zimbabwean with a passport was at it – popping over the border for a little canny shopping then returning to flog the spoils back home.

There were two problems. The second would be getting the car into Zimbabwe without paying the gazillion per cent import tax. I would cross this bridge when I came to it, by speaking to a friend of a friend of a friend – and, apparently, by slipping some Dolly Parton cassettes to a border guard named Hezekiel. The first, and more pressing, was how to pay for the car. Without credit cards, this meant cash, and the Reserve Bank of Zimbabwe set a miserly single-trip export limit of Z$400 (then about £75). Banks would not issue foreign currency, and my precious supply of sterling had already dwindled to a pittance. The car prices we'd been quoted may have been a bargain in Zimbabwean terms, but it was clear that the amount of cash we could legitimately take into Botswana would not be enough.

So, taking advice from old hands, we begged, borrowed and scraped together all the cash we could. The plan was to declare only what we could legally export and smuggle the rest over the border, secreting it about our persons. For some reason it was decided that I should be the mule; perhaps because it was I who'd hatched the idea – or, more likely, because I was the one with the largest pants. Either way, it was with heavily laden underwear that I had boarded the train at Bulawayo.

'It'll be fine,' the others had sniggered, as we pulled away from the platform. 'They're hardly going to check *down there*.' And I had relaxed, albeit a little sweatier and more uncomfortably seated than them, as we picked up speed. Soon Bulawayo's industrial western suburbs had given way to the arid bush of Matabeleland. There was no turning back.

The carriage was packed. The three of us crammed in among the other passengers. Bags were jammed into overhead racks and wedged between knees and ankles, many containing goods that their owners hoped to sell in Botswana if they could get them over the border. And it was a big 'if': customs officers had long been wise to these duty-dodging antics. A palpable tension settled on the carriage.

Dusk was falling by the time we reached the border at Plumtree, some 100 kilometres southwest of Bulawayo. As the train slowed, passengers began searching for documents, rummaging in bags, preparing for the guards. The gaunt-faced woman opposite me slid out a suitcase and removed a large pile of printed cotton wraps. With a patience born of long practice, she unfolded them one by one and, standing up, tied each in turn around her waist. By the time she sat down again she had become a very large woman with a surprisingly thin face and arms.

As soon as the train had hissed to a halt, new passengers were scrambling aboard and boys swarming along the track to hawk mealies and groundnuts through the windows. I craned out to survey the platform. Sure enough, a phalanx of starched uniforms and peaked caps was mounting the first carriage. The guards would work their way up the train, checking papers, stamping passports, collecting customs slips and searching anybody whose 'nothing to declare' didn't quite ring true.

A knot of fear tightened in my stomach. What *had* I been thinking? Of *course* they'd search me. We were the only white faces, and everybody knew young *mzungus* on public transport could only be up to no good. Smuggling ganja, probably. Besides, I break into a guilty sweat at the sight of a traffic warden. I'd surely give myself away. In fact, they probably already knew. They'd been tipped off. They were coming for me.

'Stay here,' I muttered to the others and, ignoring their looks of alarm, began shouldering my way down the aisle. The toilets. I could hide there. The door on the right was locked. But the one on the left gave way and I stumbled inside, closing it behind me and breathing hard. Safe.

Who was I kidding? *Not* safe. They'd search the toilets. Of course they would. And anyway, I'd have to get my passport stamped or they wouldn't let me into Botswana.

Heart pounding, I cast around my squalid little cell for a solution. Flush the money down the bowl? Cut it up and swallow it? Then I spied the hatch. It swung open to my trembling fingers. Eureka! With no time to lose, I dropped my jeans, pulled off my shoes and started emptying my underwear. In seconds flat I had stuffed the cash into the hatch, closed it, flushed the chain – feigned innocence – and was returning to my seat.

In the event, there were no grillings, friskings or shakedowns. We handed over our less than honest customs declarations for the polite, smiling officials. Once the last guard had disembarked, we pulled away into the night with a collective sigh of relief. We were through. Come dawn we would be rolling into Gaborone. The passengers bedded down as best they could for the hours ahead. The fat/skinny woman opposite me stood up, removed and repacked each wrap in turn then sat down again, now simply skinny again. As soon as the carriage had nodded off I would collect my stash.

But as the rustling turned to snoring, so my fears returned. What if the officers' smiles had been a charade? What if they'd found my money and were now hiding – perhaps in plain clothes – waiting to nab me when I returned to the scene of my crime? In local headlines it was always 'nab': 'Councillor nabbed for misuse of government vehicle'; 'Street vendor nabbed for selling onions without licence'; 'Expatriate teacher nabbed for being complete arse.'

So now I'm staring at the locked hatch, wracked with doubt. Is my money in there or not? Have they left it as bait? Perhaps there's a guard crouched in the toilet opposite, chuckling unpleasantly and hefting a baton in his meaty fists. What happens to currency smugglers in a Zimbabwe jail?

I creep back to break the bad news to Louise. 'What do you mean, you didn't get it?' she hisses. I daren't meet her eye but lever my backpack down from the luggage rack and fish through the outer pockets in search of something – anything – that might rescue me. Bird book, insect spray, playing cards, Swiss army knife. Bingo! Clutching my trusty weapon, I return to the loo.

I'd love to say that I locate the appropriate tool on my knife immediately and whip off the hatch's hinges before you can say 'unexplained death in police custody'. But it takes ten minutes of grunting, swearing, twisting, chiselling and splitting before – bleeding from a gashed thumb – I've inflicted sufficient damage on the lock for the door to concede defeat and flop open.

And there's my cash. All bundled up in plastic bands, just how I left it. I fish out the grubby wads and stuff them back down my pants. Then, heart in mouth, I open the toilet door and step out into the corridor.

There's nobody there. Nobody to bludgeon me senseless, clap me in irons and drag me away: just the reassuring rhythm of the train on the tracks and its snoring passengers. I'm drained, shaking with relief and adrenalin, but elated. I'm the daredevil master criminal who's just blown the safe of Mr Big.

I strut back down the carriage, barging through legs and luggage with all the swagger of a man who knows he carries in his capacious underpants a shiny secondhand Mazda 323 – or at least the cash equivalent. I'm a travel-hardened criminal and Africa is my oyster.

Mike Unwin is the author of several books for Bradt, including *Swaziland* and *Southern African Wildlife*, and writes regularly for such publications as *The Independent*, *BBC Wildlife* and *Wanderlust*. In 2013 he was voted UK Travel Writer of the Year by the British Guild of Travel  Writers. Before becoming a freelance writer, Mike worked for eight years in southern Africa, first as a teacher in Zimbabwe and later as a publisher in Swaziland. Today, when venturing out from his home on England's south coast, he tries to travel a little more responsibly – but old habits die hard.

Stranded in the Skerries
Nicky Gardner

Remote island communities often come with their own soundtrack. In low latitudes it may be the rattle of cicadas, eclipsed further north by the screech of gulls. But cast back to the last century and another sound was a signal reminder of remoteness: the hum of generators.

I have over the years learned to distinguish the hum of a Cummins from a Caterpillar, a Pramac from a Perkins. In urban settings, the constant hum of generators is often a sharp reminder of the failure of government to invest adequately in infrastructure. But shift to offshore islands, and that noise of generators is a true sign of remoteness, a mark of a community that is so far from civilisation that it must fend for itself.

In the autumn of 1983, the generators on the Out Skerries fell silent, and the hum that had for decades defined the rhythm of island life was no more. The feisty Scottish nationalist politician Winnie Ewing visited the Skerries and, with a flick of a switch, she connected the islanders to the UK national grid. No-one gave greater thanks for the new arrangements than Charlie Hughson, a lifelong resident of the Skerries who had lost an arm in an accident with a diesel generator.

The fate of island communities is often captured in a single person. In St Kilda, the death in 1930 of Mary Gillies from appendicitis helped crystallise the difficult decision that the entire St Kilda community would forsake their island home and move to the mainland. The matter of Charlie's arm prompted no thoughts of evacuation from the Skerries, but it did encourage the islanders to ponder the benefits of connectivity. Charlie's suffering was all the worse because the poor man had to endure a three-hour crossing by boat in fearfully stormy seas to hospital in Lerwick, the main town on the Shetland mainland.

Thus the islanders petitioned for an airstrip and a more reliable ferry link. They came in 1983 along with mains electricity. Linking the Skerries into the Scottish air ambulance network meant that none of the residents should ever again have to endure such terrible discomfort as Charlie Hughson.

It was with the air ambulance plane that I made my first visit to the Out Skerries. Eddie Watt was at the controls of the Britten-Norman Islander as we took off from the airfield at Tingwall on the Shetland mainland, and set a northeasterly course.

I had a sense of unease about the whole venture. Are not islands after all meant to be visited by boat? As a principled devotee of slow travel, I was deeply aware of breaking my own rules. Yet here I was, taking to the skies for a twenty-minute flight to the Out Skerries.

I had travelled over half a continent by train, bus and ferry to be in Shetland to speak at a dinner on the theme of slow travel. Old friends had invited me. I had hesitated, then eventually said yes, speculating that there might just be time to fit in a quick visit to one of the smaller islands in the Shetlands that I had never set foot on: Foula, Fair Isle or the Out Skerries.

My journey had spread over two full days and nights, concluding with a long ferry journey from Aberdeen to Shetland. My talk had been written, rewritten and rehearsed – a few fluent thoughts on why slow travel makes sense, backed up by a handful of happy anecdotes about tapping the pulse of rural communities by taking slow options. There was a little subtext about the virtues of not flying too often. Journeys are not things to be rushed.

A free day in the islands, and a sunny one at that, is something to be treasured. The Out Skerries beckoned. My first choice would naturally have been to take the boat. I quickly discovered, however, that the ferry schedules were not designed for anyone wanting to make a day trip – at least not on a Thursday. The timetables were for Skerries-based fishermen wanting to ship their catch over to Lerwick for onward transfer to the fish markets on the Scottish mainland, and a Thursday was not the right day to choose to leave from Vidlin. So I had opted for a quick out-and-back journey by plane. The schedule would have me back on the Shetland mainland by late afternoon, in good time for my evening commitment.

These flights on tiny aircraft are a world apart from mainstream aviation. Loganair was the operator in those days, and using the air ambulance plane for short scheduled flights around the islands is a good way of keeping costs down. The sun shone as Eddie flew us low over a thousand tiny islets: Muckle Fladdicap down below us to the left, Flaeshans of Rumble to our right, then the little island of Filla.

'After dropping you off on the Skerries, I'm flying back to Tingwall, then down to Fair Isle,' Eddie said. 'I'll be back at the Skerries to pick you up at 4.30 p.m. Just be at the airstrip a few minutes before that.' The arrangements seemed perfect. I'd have time to get changed and be at the dinner venue by 6.30 p.m.

'You'll hear me coming anyway,' Eddie added. I knew what he meant. The noise of the twin-engined Islander is as distinctive as a Perkins generator.

Soon we were banking over Grunay, part of the Out Skerries group, and a good reminder of just how fragile human settlement is in this remote region. No-one has lived on Grunay for years, but gazing down from the plane I could see the remains of a neat row of cottages once used by the lighthouse keepers and their families. In the middle of the island, I could detect evidence of a walled vegetable garden. Nature was reclaiming the space where once tough and rugged individualists tilled their potato beds.

With Grunay uninhabited since the lighthouse was automated, Skerries life is now concentrated on two islands linked by a bridge: Housay (or West Isle) and Bruray (or East Isle). It was on Bruray that we came in to land.

Eddie waved and the Islander climbed into the clear skies. I walked from the airstrip down towards the pier, confident that in seven hours I could roam over both islands and get a feel for life in the Skerries. Within a few minutes, I had met Charlie Hughson (who is naturally more recognisable than many of the other seventy-nine inhabitants of the islands), found and tested the local telephone booth and discovered that the Skerries possess the finest public conveniences that I have ever encountered.

By early afternoon, little wisps of mist were beginning to drape the higher hills on the north side of Housay and Bruray. Within an hour, the sun was tussling with the *haar* and it was very clear that the sun was losing the battle. Soon the Skerries were draped in fog. By four I was sitting on Jampie's Hill, the nearby airstrip hardly discernible in the mist. I heard the rumble of the approaching plane, heard it circling overhead for twenty minutes and then heard it receding away to the west. Eddie had evidently decided that a landing was not possible.

There are few travel dilemmas that cannot be resolved by chocolate, so I walked down to the island shop on the shore of Böd Voe, pondering along the way the bad luck that had left me stranded on the Skerries. Equipped with the necessary rations for an improvised overnight stay, and fortified by a KitKat, I walked anxiously along to the phone box.

'Niall, is that you? This is Nicky. Look, about the event this evening. The dinner.'

Niall is a perceptive man and could immediately sense there was a problem. 'Something up then, Nicky?' he asked.

'No, no, the talk's all done and dusted. Loaded and ready to go. But yes, Niall. There is something. Remember I told you I hardly ever go on planes. Well, look, I'm over in the Out Skerries. Came here for the day.'

'Aha,' said Niall slowly, as it dawned on him that his celebrated exponent of slow travel was a little flexible with her principles. 'So you did nae reckon with the haar,' he observed with a touch of sympathy in his voice. 'Well, we cannae cancel the dinner. We'll just have to go ahead without you.'

Niall was there to meet me on the pier at Vidlin on the Shetland mainland as I stepped off the *MV Filla* in bright sunshine the following day. 'Here, look, I've brought you a Shetland souvenir,' he said, passing me a copy of the menu from the previous evening's dinner. It had been signed by some of the dinner guests, most of them adding wry comments about the merits of slow travel.

'Fresh Shetland mackerel paté with almond pesto. Duo of Shetland monkfish and fillet of salmon,' I read out loud.

'And you, Nicky? Had a good evening, did you?' asked Niall with a smile.

I mentioned that I had much enjoyed the apple that was my supper and that a night spent sleeping in the Skerries chapel was surprisingly comfortable. I told of how the haar had lifted and I had walked in the late evening up to the highest point on Bruray. There I had sat, watching the stars, and considering whether I would one day grow up and start behaving responsibly. This is a question I still ponder, but irresponsibility brings its own rewards.

I had gone to the Skerries on a whim and, as travel disasters go, it was only a modest misadventure. It had been fun. On a dawn walk around West Voe I'd watched the seals taking their morning exercise. I was even neat and tidy, having showered by the pier, where those fabulous public loos had a real shower (provided as a convenience to the crews of visiting boats).

Travelling on a whim has become a rare luxury, and that has much to do with our affection for flying. Journeys are planned in every detail, so much so that they lose all spontaneity. The best journeys I have made have been those that were less rehearsed, the ones that were improvised and uncertain. What pleasure can there be in travel when you know a warm feather bed awaits at the end of the day?

These are issues that Niall and I discussed as he drove me down to Lerwick to catch the ferry to Aberdeen. 'You're still going home the slow way? Ferries and trains?' he asked. 'Or should I take you to the airport?'

'I'll stick to the slow option,' I said with a smile.

Nicky Gardner is a Berlin-based travel writer. She is co-editor of *hidden europe* magazine (www.hiddeneurope.co.uk). Nicky is also the author of *A Manifesto for Slow Travel*, published by *hidden europe* in 2009.

The Casualty and the Priest
Ben Fogle

Let's be honest: we Western travellers can be a little bit arrogant. The simple fact we can afford to travel to wild, remote places, where poverty can be rife, is arguably a form of arrogance. The fact that we are from a developed country, and by and large 'wealthier', often gives us advantages not afforded to the native population. We all try to be good, responsible travellers but just occasionally the assumption that we can do what we want can get us in all sorts of trouble.

I was four weeks into an eight-week film shoot in South America. I had begun with an attempted ascent of Chimborazo in Ecuador followed by a two-week journey into the hot, steamy bowels of the deepest canyon on earth, the 3,354 metre deep Cotahausi Canyon in Peru. I was already weary from weeks of trekking and I had the prospect of two further expeditions in succession. I had been struck with an unidentified lurgy for several days and wasn't feeling my best. I had just a day to get out of the canyon and back to Cusco before heading on to meet my next film crew and volunteers in Santiago, Chile before heading to the Atacama Desert. Timing was crucial.

The team and crew were elated: we had reached the lost city of Marpa and they were all heading home. We boarded the bus and set off on the long twelve-hour journey to Cusco. We had been driving for several hours when the bus stopped behind a queue of cars. Dozens of people milled around the roadside and the tail of traffic disappeared into the horizon.

'*Huelga, huelga,*' shouted someone. 'Strike, strike.'

We stepped from the bus and wandered alongside the stationary traffic to try to see what was happening. Ten, twenty, thirty minutes later and we were still walking past buses, cars, trucks, motorbikes. It was the biggest traffic jam I have ever seen in my life, the vehicles all spilling their human contents on to the side of the road. Tents had been erected and stalls set up to sell food. To be honest, it didn't look good. It was like a refugee camp. Babies screamed in the arms of their exasperated mothers. Occasionally a driver honked a horn fruitlessly. There were hundreds – perhaps thousands – of vehicles snaking along the mountain road. And at the very back was our little bus.

Eventually we reached a bridge crossing a river. It had been partly disassembled and huge boulders had been rolled into the middle to make a strong barricade. On the other side of the river were similar scenes of traffic wretchedness. Two noisy groups of Peruvians held banners on both sides of the bridge and chanted in unison. They were the protesters. They had been there for nearly a week and they weren't going anywhere. The bridge was impassable.

'Is there any way we can cross the river?' we asked a rather harassed-looking official. He shook his head gloomily. He explained that every bridge for a hundred miles had been blocked. We were at an impasse. If we stayed we would merely be joining the longest traffic jam in the world and risked being stuck for a further week.

We began the long walk back to the bus. I had a whole team of people waiting for me in Cusco. Without the presenter, the show couldn't go on. The clock was ticking. I was tired and felt rotten. We must be able to do something, I thought. That was the arrogance speaking, you see.

We got back to the bus and explained our predicament. Food and water were becoming scarce and rumour had it that the army was soon to be drafted in to keep the peace. As far as we understood, the strike was over a rise in bus fares. The locals were fed up of paying above inflation rises and had quite understandably made the lives of other road users impossible. While I sympathised with their plight, I really wished they could have picked a different week.

I sat on the bus, hatching a plan. What if we HAVE to cross that bridge, as in an emergency, I pondered. My eyes settled on the large first aid kit. We didn't have a casualty. So we would make one. No-one volunteered to break a bone for us so we set about faking a casualty. It was perhaps slightly insensitive but at the time it seemed genius.

One of my team, Ann, volunteered to be our casualty. We giggled as we wrapped her in bandages doused in iodine and some leftover Heinz ketchup. We smeared some talc on to her face to give it a pallid tone and then we inserted a dummy needle beneath a piece of gauze and attached a drip. It looked pretty convincing, even if I say so myself.

At this point, the driver was dispatched to speak to the strikers and negotiate a passage through. It sounded so easy. 'She's dying,' he pleaded with tears in his eyes. That was perhaps a little more dramatic than we had planned. But it worked. The good, Catholic people of Peru weren't prepared to let a fellow human being die, even if it meant breaking the blockade. Before we knew it our bus was being ushered past vehicle after vehicle. Meanwhile everyone from the strikers to the poor people caught in the jam had been drafted in to remove the blockade and repair the bridge so that we could pass. It was like the parting of the Red Sea. We all sat in the bus, smug but hiding our smirks behind concerned looks. We were genius. It was worthy of an Oscar.

Until the priest boarded the bus. 'My dear children, I am so sorry,' he lamented with his American accent. He had been living with the local community for several years and had heard about Ann.

Holding his rosary beads he started reading Ann her last rites.

'I shall come with you to the hospital,' he continued.

'We've been striking for a week,' he explained. 'These people have nothing.

This is their last hope, their last chance to make the government listen.'

I began to sweat. My smirk faded as I realised what we had done. Unethical and now unholy. This was not how I had planned it. Not only had we lied to the people but we were now stuck with a fake casualty and a real priest. I looked around the bus at the horrified faces. We were going to hell.

It's amazing how events can spiral out of control. What had seemed like such a simple ruse had now put us in a singularly difficult situation. Should we carry on the deception all the way to the hospital? What would happen when the doctors uncovered the fake drip and the tomato sauce?

Call it divine intervention (not that we deserved it), but as we passed the miles of traffic on the other side, a young boy came dashing to the bus. 'Padre, padre!' he shouted at the priest. His mother was really dying and they needed him.

'Go, father,' I implored. 'We'll be fine.'

And with that he disappeared.

It was a quiet journey back to Cusco. We might have outwitted the locals and their strike, but God had the last laugh. Call it schadenfreude, or just poor luck, but I left Peru with more than just a guilty conscience. It was here that I picked up a tropical disease, Leishmaniasis, and ended up in hospital for several months.

The moral of the story: don't try to be so smart.

Ben Fogle is a presenter, writer and adventurer. His achievements include rowing the 3,500 miles across the Atlantic Ocean, crossing Antarctica on foot and walking across the Empty Quarter of the Middle East, as well as completing the infamous Marathon des Sables, a 180-mile marathon across the Sahara Desert. He has presented  numerous BBC programmes, including *Swimming with Crocodiles*, *Extreme Dreams*, *The Secrets of Scott's Hut* and *Wild in Africa*. He writes weekly for *The Sunday Telegraph*, contributes to other publications including *The New York Times* and has written seven bestselling books, the latest being *The Accidental Naturalist*. He is an ambassador for WWF, Médecins Sans Frontières and Tusk.

The Long March
Jennifer Barclay

Maybe it had something to do with the combat trousers Gav and I picked up army surplus on the market in Seoul, but we seemed to be on a mission to rough it across China: to do China hardcore. It certainly had something to do with the budget. We'd blown half of it in a week in Japan, and now had to tighten our belts. On our new, no-nonsense trousers.

We'd taken a container ship from Incheon to Shanghai, via a two-day typhoon in the East China Sea. It seemed a good start. A few days later, we boarded a westbound train, travelling 'hard sleeper' in bunks complete with cockroaches. In Wuhan, sitting at street stalls in warm sunshine, we watched shirtless men conjure clouds of fragrant steam from sizzling woks, and practised the words for 'thank you' and 'beer' (try as we might, we still hadn't mastered the word for 'toilet', resorting to embarrassing charades). Taking local transport and avoiding anything that smacked of organised sightseeing, travelling by the seat of our combat pants, would lead, we sensed, to unforgettable experiences.

Our goal was to cross China from east to west, getting a feel for the country away from its showcase cities, and ending up at one of the country's great natural wonders, Hailuogou Glacier Park, where we hoped to glimpse Gongga Shan, the highest mountain east of the Himalayas.

When we saw the boat we were taking up the River Yangtze, our hearts sank. The regular passenger ferry was old, rusty and dilapidated. Up a greasy staircase and across a wet hallway, our second-class cabin rattled and hummed with the engine's vibrations. There were smears of what looked like blood on the window frame. The red carpet was mottled black with years of spitting and gum and cigarette burns. In a nice touch, the management had left a dead cockroach under my pillow.

Still, it was only for five days.

Embarking on China's great river, we watched narrow cargo craft and fishing barges, laundry sailing from bamboo poles, as they navigated waters the colour of milky coffee. Our boat transformed itself into an ersatz floating casino as the staff snapped down mah-jong tiles in a haze of smoke in the 'OK Lounge'; it sounded like an apology – sure, it's not a *great* lounge, but it's OK. We slept with sleeping bags covering our heads as cockroaches streamed across the cabin walls, and lived in fear of the toilets where you squatted over a communal trough washed by a flow of river water.

But as the days passed, massive mountains began to rise on either side, dwarfing even the swanky Three Gorges cruise ships that plied the river. People carried goods up and down the slopes in baskets on their backs. Hundreds of steps led up to blackened old towns. The landscape changed from stark canyons with gaping caves and rocks eroded into fantastical shapes, to lush greenery and waterfalls, and farms with cattle and ragged banana trees. A young boy held the motor of a wooden canoe, his dog standing at the helm. I was mesmerised by the rural landscape, soon to be submerged when the gorges would be flooded by a large dam in the name of progress.

Leaving the river at Chongqing, we continued west. The town of Leshan had cleverly made it impossible to see one of the biggest rock carvings of Buddha in the world without paying a hefty entrance fee; capitalism was alive and well all across the new China. In a town where the beeping of car horns woke us in the morning like a flock of noisy geese, and the staff woke us again by knocking at the door to ask if we wanted anything (once knocking to let us know we'd left the 'do not disturb' sign on the door), in a moment of foolishness we'd gone to the zoo, and had been encouraged to pet a tame panda while the keeper, waving his cigarette, put a carrot in its mouth and told us to take a photo.

'Don't be scared!' said the keeper. It wasn't the panda I was scared of.

Finally, we were at the last stage of our journey across the country. We squished into a van, and made our way to Moxi via roads half-destroyed by landslides and rockfalls. This was about as far west as you could go before Tibet, and the closest village to the glacier park.

It had been raining in Moxi, and the roads were mud, which combined with the wooden shops to give the main street a medieval air, especially the butcher's shop with carcasses hanging from hooks over the doorstep. We were sitting outside the building where Mao stayed during his Long March when we met the Danes. They were the first Westerners we'd seen in a week. We all looked at one another in surprise.

'Beer?' suggested Gav.

The Danes, Mikkel and Helene, were also in Moxi to see the mountains and glaciers. The problem was that Hailuogou Glacier Park was now geared up for tour groups. Not so long ago, it had been possible to trek up the mountain with horses, stopping at rustic refuges along the way; instead, we had to take the shuttle bus with groups of holiday-making Chinese businessmen. Although the stops were still called 'camps', the refuges had been torn down to make way for resorts like the delightfully named Hailuogou Hotsprings Holiday Hamlet and, at the top, a big, new hotel.

It was raining and cold. After weeks of backpacking and sleeping with the cockroaches, we self-consciously dripped our way across the marble lobby to reception, where it was confirmed that the price of a room was somewhat beyond our means. But where else could we stay the night? Eventually, for a still-hefty price, the four of us were allowed to line up our sleeping bags like sardines in an empty storage room. We went to warm up in the bar.

Next morning, a light snow was falling as we tramped through fragrant forest up the misty trail. At the end of it, partially hidden by cloud, loomed the magnificent snowy peak of Gongga Shan, over 7,500 metres. Below, the pale grey glacier tongue stretched down into dense forest. From the viewing platform, like a parody of Victorian-era British gentry, rich Chinese tourists were paying to be carried down on to the glacier on stretcher-style bamboo litters.

We knew that the 'done way' to appreciate nature in Asia was en masse from the designated 'Number One Scenic Viewpoint' at the designated optimal hour, preferably when the peak would resemble a phoenix or dragon and make an ideal backdrop for a romantic photograph. Being Westerners and, what's more, no softies, we preferred to approach things somewhat differently. So we voted not to hire a guide, but to enjoy the wilderness alone.

Mikkel and Helene had that Danish air of being sensible outdoors types; Helene's father was a renowned mountain-climber. Gav and I didn't exactly fit into the category of sensible outdoors types, but the army surplus gear gave us credibility and made us feel capable. We'd take our wilderness unpackaged, raw, no being herded around. In fact, we could walk all the way down the glacier, cross the tiny stream at the bottom, and return up the forested slopes to the hotel. A plan was formed.

As we marched down the path, we gradually realised that those tiny dots we'd seen from above were actually people, and what had seemed mere ridges on the ice revealed themselves to be huge, wave-like crevasses. The tour groups receded; awe-inspiring cracks in the ice surrounded us. We clambered over the ice, admiring its strange shapes, peering into dark holes that plummeted seemingly without end. We walked and climbed across the empty glacier with the great snowy mountain towering above.

This was real travel, we congratulated ourselves, this was what we'd come here for. We climbed, ached, and wondered idly how much further it might be. Up close, everything was bigger than we'd originally thought.

'I'm pretty sure we're close,' said Gav. 'It's just over that next ridge. Another twenty minutes at the most.' As the day wore on, we understood there was no turning back. 'Just over that next ridge,' became a running joke. And it got less and less funny.

When finally, exhausted and flagging, we reached the tip of the glacier tongue, that tiny stream now revealed itself to be a fast-flowing river beneath cliffs of ice.

However we looked at the problem, we couldn't see a way around it. With the route to the hotel on the other side of the river, and nothing but pristine forest surrounding us, there was no alternative. Gingerly, we made our way down the cliffs to the 'stream', and then, removing shoes and socks and holding on to one another, we waded in, the icy water freezing our feet.

I am one of those people whose fingers go numb in damp cold; I get chilblains on my toes from stone floors in the south of France. So while I'm pretty sure I'm the only person who actually cried, let's just say it wasn't an experience any of us wanted to repeat. Gav, the hero, carried me the last part of the way.

Later, we learned how dangerous a river at the foot of a glacier can be. Even a small iceberg falling off into the water could have spelt disaster. But apart from the aching cold, we survived unscathed and trudged up the hill, all the way back to our sardine-tin at the hotel. The staff had opened the window again to let in the bracing air.

Next day, we caught the bus down to the Hailuogou Hotsprings Holiday Hamlet and lounged in thermal pools while the Chinese tourists threw their empty cigarette packets on to the ground around us. At dinner we watched the hotel staff don traditional costumes over their jeans to become Tibetan Dancing Girls. And we laughed, as only survivors can.

Jennifer Barclay is the author of *Falling in Honey* and *Meeting Mr Kim*, editor of *The Traveller's Friend* and co-editor of *AWOL: Tales for Travel-Inspired Minds*. Originally from England, she has lived in Canada, France and Greece, and – when not on a long walk – can often be found at www.octopus-in-my-ouzo.blogspot.com.

April 13: Kangchung Himal Camp 17,700 feet

Phil Deutschle

Bebeep, bebeep... My watch alarm sounds from the side-wall pocket. At 3.30 a.m., it's cold and dark. Wind shakes the tent, but it's not strong enough to worry about. I light the stove in the vestibule and it goes to work warming the tent and melting the snow that I collected last night. As the temperature rises, so does my activity: stuffing odds and ends into my pack, eating granola with warm milk, melting more snow to carry on the ascent, pulling on my thick socks, and finally lacing up my boots. All this takes one-and-a-quarter hours and I'm soon moving up the glacier...

I plunge my ice axe into the slope and lean forward for a short rest. I'm already halfway to the low point between the two peaks, halfway to the col. I've opted for the route up the right side and it's been a good choice. So far I've met only step-over crevasses. My plan is to traverse to the centre of the glacier just below the section of ice blocks.

I continue up and step over another crevasse. I dismiss the ever-present danger of falling into a crevasse that's concealed by snow. The climbing is pleasant. The surface of the glacier is firm and my crampons bite securely with each step. I encounter only small patches of hard ice. A few small clouds hang over the Chikim La and the wind has stopped.

Suddenly I see a movement and I jerk my head up. An ice block the size of two railroad cars slowly topples over. It picks up speed and the sound comes a moment later – a deep groan and crunch, like a train crash in slow motion. The falling ice creates its own wind and a cloud of snow billows up.

I'm directly below the avalanche, but where should I go? I have the crazy notion that I can dodge whatever comes my way – like dodging a tidal wave? The falling ice consumes everything in its path.

As I realise the hopelessness of my situation, the entire avalanche begins to sink, plunging into a chasm just above my proposed traverse. Ice missiles the size of footballs whizz by, but only the smallest pieces hit me. The glacier shakes and grumbles as the ice drops into its bowels. I'm awed and intimidated.

With nowhere to go but up, I continue climbing. Just below the scene of the avalanche is a ramp leading to the left, towards the centre of the glacier. It gives me some tense moments. I move swiftly along a line of ice blocks and I stop to rest when I'm above the icefall.

From the top of the col, I look down on the Gyubanare Glacier and across to Tibet, four miles distant. The east summit of Kangchung looms 1,500 feet above. The face is steep and featureless, so I contour around the col towards the north ridge. The pointed summit looks broken at the very top and I'm unenthusiastic about making a nearly complete climb.

The north ridge is steeper than I had expected, and I'm soon stopped by a crevasse. I traverse to the right, climbing far across the face before I can skirt around it. Instead of returning to the ridge, I proceed straight up, using the inside points of my crampons and the pick of my ice axe. The angle is severe, and I feel very exposed.

Another crevasse divides the face. It's bottomless and its sides taper in a deep, cold blue. Because of the steep slope, the crevasse's near edge forms an acute angle and its far edge is almost directly above. I could balance on the near edge, step over the crevasse, and continue on the face above. But if I slip, the game is over. I decide to traverse around this one too. I hold the lip of the crevasse like a guardrail and, keeping my right hand on the axe, I confidently begin. After two steps, I FALL! My body pendulums across the ice and my feet swing through the air. Suddenly I'm hanging by my arms, one hand holding the lip of ice and the other hand clutching the axe. I kick in my front points and pull myself up. I regain my footing, but not my confidence. I had slipped. *Slipped?* I stand motionless for five minutes, pondering the steep ice and my near fall to oblivion. Reluctantly I start down. Slowly. Descending the slope is awkward, and I'm acutely aware of the exposure.

Back on the col, I eat a chocolate bar while I assess the prospects. The west peak looks easier. Its summit is forty-six feet lower than the east peak, putting it just under 20,000 feet, but it's certainly a challenge. I'll be pressed for time, and I warn myself to start down by 1.30 p.m. or risk losing my way in the dark.

I recross the col and start up the steepening and narrowing ridge of the west peak. My progress is good and I encounter no crevasses. After an hour of steep climbing, the ridge narrows to an arête of ice too thin to stand on. I straddle it with a leg on each side, like a child trying to slide up a banister. There must be a better way.

Passing this, the ridge broadens and then ends in a magnificent rock cliff. Removing my crampons and overboots, I scramble down and around. As I climb along the bottom of the cliff, I spot a route of descent that would circumvent a return to the glacier. I'll have to find just the right rock chute; the others all terminate in cliffs.

Back on the ridge proper, I look up at the apparent summit, but remembering the view from the col, I know that it's just a levelling of the ridge. The deep snow makes for hard climbing, but this is offset by the sight of Everest rising far above the other peaks. The Chinese northwest face is completely exposed.

Reaching the false summit at 1.15 p.m., I eat another chocolate bar and take the day's first squat-down rest. With wool gloves and nylon overmitts off, I photograph Everest and then change the film before resuming the climb.

The ridge is less steep than further down, but the softer snow is exhausting. My time limit expires and I have no thoughts of turning back.

Keeping clear of a cornice, I slog higher and see the end. It's not the summit, just the end. The route is blocked by a crevasse and an overhanging wall of ice. The crevasse ends to the left and is replaced by a drop of vertical ice – broken and dangerous. The crevasse continues to the right, though the slope on the far side is climbable. I could jump it, but the lip is undercut and unstable. I look back and forth between the possibilities, each becoming more frightful with every glance.

Impulsively I start to the left, committing myself before my growing fear forces me down. I traverse directly out and around, cursing myself for not taking a rest before beginning; I'm already worn out. The ice is bad and I try not to look down. With each step, pieces of ice break loose and hurl themselves down the face. I reach the point from which I hope to climb up and regain the crest of the ridge. With laborious swings of the axe, I chop out a shelf that gives me a space to stand with both feet while I catch my breath. The ridge top is close, but from here up the ice is all hard and fragmented.

Standing on the pseudo-security of my little ledge, I hack out the first eight steps and then begin up. As I move higher and become more tired, the steps I cut become smaller and more precarious. The chipped-out pieces of ice fall away noiselessly. I forgo chopping holds on the final six feet, and decide to use the last of my strength to pull myself on to the crest. My lungs pump for oxygen as I stand in my topmost steps. I jab the pick of the axe into the ice on the top, then praying that it'll hold, I pull up. My hands clutch the axe and my feet tiptoe higher, till I can swing my right leg over the crest and on to the snow of the far side. Except there is no far side; my leg finds nothing!

I have climbed the side of a wafer of ice and I kneel on the edge, which is just wide enough for my two knees. My hands still cling to the axe, but my body slides down the arête as it crumbles beneath my weight. It will hold only minutes longer and I know it's the end. They'll find my tent and nothing more.

Damn it Phil, climb! I try to pull myself up the arête, but nothing happens. I'm physically done in and I'm terrified of breaking away more ice. *Pull, damn it. Pull!!* This time I manage to shift my knees a bit. A section of ice falls to the right. Again I pull, bringing my knees up to my hands. This amount of progress lessens my fear, though I still crouch like a child. I gingerly kick in my front points, one foot at a time, then I pull out the axe and drive it in further along. I creep and pull, bringing myself up to the axe, and in this way – like an inchworm – I move along the arête.

Further up, the ice widens and becomes more stable. I stand, and continue upward towards the summit.

Again in heavy snow, I step to the top of a rise and look around. The mountain has another lump some distance further, but this one seems higher. I'm on the summit, so I do what's expected of me. Setting the camera with the self-timer, I sit in the snow and the shutter clicks.

Elsewhere in the world, a 19,977-foot peak would be an important mountain, but here it's insignificant. This is possibly Kangchung West's first ascent, and certainly its first solo ascent. I feel no elation, only numbness and exhaustion. I look at my watch, but I don't see the time. I only know that it's late – too late to get back in the light. I don't even know *how* I'll get down. It doesn't really matter. I wonder why I didn't fall back there. One of those peaks to the north must be Cho Oyu, but Everest is truncated by the clouds.

I stay ten minutes and start down, towards the east face. I don't think or ponder over this decision; I just go. The face is very steep, but the snow is soft. I climb facing out by kicking backwards with my heels to make steps. I'll descend the face to the col and then return to camp. *In the dark? Down a crevassed glacier?* Maybe I'll dig in for the night.

Not expecting to make it, I lower myself one step at a time, down and down. The slope worsens, giving a scary view toward the Gyubanare Glacier. I'm stopped by a rocky band of cliffs and I'm forced to traverse to my right, towards my ascent route. The entire face is vertically corrugated into mammoth waves, so every ten yards I must claw my way through and around a crest of ice. I take no time to be careful. What difference does it make? It's just a matter of falling rather than freezing. I promise myself that I'll never climb solo again.

My full attention is focused on stepping and balancing, and I'm startled to find tracks in the snow. It's the false summit where I ate a chocolate bar a lifetime ago.

A reassuring line of tracks points the way home. I follow, cautiously now, hoping to find that rock chute that I spotted on the way up. I pause only once – taking off my snow goggles to better see those faint, encouraging ice-axe holes and crampon marks. Despite this, I lose my way in the growing clouds and darkness. I try to stay in the light areas that mean snow and away from the dark ones that mean rock as I head down the south buttress in the general direction of camp.

I saunter dreamily down the middle of a tributary glacier that I suspect to be close to the bottom. I'm abruptly awakened when a large section of ice drops a metre beneath me. Unhurt, I climb to the moraine and away from the danger. Looking over the moraine's crest, I see the small frozen lake where my tent stands. I skirt the shore and reach camp under a starless sky.

Phil Deutschle is author of *The Two-Year Mountain* (Bradt), which chronicles his life as a Peace Corps Volunteer in Nepal in the 1970s plus an emotional return there 34 years later. The extract above is the story of his reckless solo attempt on a Himalayan peak that unbeknownst to him had  only one recorded successful ascent (by Sir Edmund Hillary's Everest team). Phil's first feature-length documentary, *Searching For Nepal*, is near completion.

The Rum Diary
Phoebe Smith

O utside, someone was screaming. Through the sound of water battering against my window – as though a waterfall had suddenly appeared on the roof and torrentially spurted across it in bucketloads – I could hear the distinct sound of human crying. This wasn't at all as I'd pictured it...

Her name was Rita. And when I first heard she was on the way to Cuba I was excited at the prospect of her paying a visit. She sounded like a force to be reckoned with – powerful and scary – but something about witnessing her strength first hand was terribly exciting. Considering all the commotion her sister Katrina had caused it was a foolhardy attitude to say the least, especially seeing as both these ladies were Category 5 hurricanes and people's lives and livelihoods were at stake. But I blame the rum.

For three days I'd been holed up in a resort in Varadero. It was my first attempt at staying at an all-inclusive hotel and by day two I was already counting down the hours until I would catch a bus to Havana and spend the rest of my week in the 'real' Cuba, away from endless greasy meals, sun lounger arguments over whether or not a crumpled towel ever constitutes a fair save, and a rather odd male Britney Spears impersonator. To cope with the enforced luxury of this sedentary holiday I had hit the bar, hard. I would strike up conversations with the maids and receptionists, and chat away to the barmen, desperate to hear about something of the world that lay beyond the compound I'd booked myself into, but all they wanted to do was help me get more food and drink.

'So tell me about where you live?' I would ask.

'It's about three hours from here... Would you like something more to drink?' they would typically reply.

'I want to know about you,' I'd persist.

'Perhaps some ice cream?'

'Tell me about your life!' I would demand.

'Here have a cocktail, ma'am,' and a drink boasting a name that promised excitement like the 'Cuban love zinger' would be presented to me as they made their escape to another waiting punter, all too easily placated with a bucket of booze.

I soon gave up trying to learn more about the country from this five-star corner and simply surrendered to the horror of the all-inclusive, safe in the knowledge that in just twenty-four more hours I would be free from it all.

It was September and the amount of money I'd had to part with to get me here from Canada, where I was working at the time, seemed ridiculously cheap. Back in 2005, with the exchange rate what it was, I had secured a weeklong trip to this Caribbean idyll for around £350 – including flights. There was a catch of course: I would be travelling in the middle of hurricane season. No problem, I had thought. Won't happen to me I told myself as I checked in to my flight at Toronto. Never. Going. To happen. So I reassured no-one in particular as the bus delivered me safely to my hotel a couple of hours later. Deliciously irresponsible of me – I practically glowed with self-assured glee as I arrived, convinced I had outwitted Mother Nature and got the steal of the century.

But then a rumour started. I first heard her name whispered by one of the reps as they deposited another busload of tourists. Rita was coming... and this lady apparently meant business.

I knew a tropical storm had been brewing before I'd left the mainland, and dismissed it as something small that would fizzle out. But what had first been caused by no more than a tropical wave that formed off the coast of west Africa had been building as it travelled. Near the Bahamas it formed into a storm and now, as it hit the warm water, it was beginning to intensify – fast. While I still dismissed the growing talk amongst the staff about Rita's arrival as idle chit-chat – just as we Brits like to talk about the weather in lieu of more exciting conversation – she was moving in a westerly direction and making a beeline for the northern coast of Cuba. The same northern coast of Cuba where I was now drinking copious amounts of rum.

Blissful in my ignorance, I ended the night sitting on a lounger near the sea, watching with a mild curiosity the darkening clouds, which now seemed to be moving rather fast overhead. I supped at my rum punch, happy that tomorrow I would head west to Havana. I slept dreaming of being swept off my feet in a salsa bar, surrounded by a cheering crowd of strangers snug against walls as yellow as burnt butter from the cigar tobacco that filled the air…

Jolting me from my dream was a knock at the door. It wasn't the usual tap of housekeeping, the soft rat-a-tat that oozed friendliness and hospitality. This one was urgent, demanding, frantic even. I stood up and walked over to the window. Slowly, in my half-awoken state, I moved the curtain to one side.

The sky was black. Not just overcast, but dim and shadowy like nightfall. I looked over to the bedside clock: 7.05 a.m. It should have been light by now. The knock came again. Then again, this time followed by a call, 'Hello – housekeeping – I am coming in!'

Everything was still for a second. Then, suddenly, there was chaos. The chambermaid burst through the door, a jacket draped around her shoulders. The zip was broken and she clasped her hood tightly to her head. It was only then I realised that it was raining.

'No worry about, only storm,' she said then thrust a plastic bag into my hands along with two bottles of water. I looked inside it. Two hard-boiled eggs, a couple of cakes, some bread, cold cuts of meat, a bit of cheese and a small bottle of rum: a food parcel.

'No breakfast – no lunch,' she said as she rushed over to my balcony doors and proceeded to secure them with crosses made from what appeared to be masking tape.

I watched agog, wondering exactly what I should do next. But my brain didn't seem to be working properly. As she started on the second window her roll of tape ran out, making it less of an X and more of a Y shape on the glass. She looked like she might say something, but thinking better of it – likely not having the necessary English to explain – she simply turned around and walked to the door.

Then as an afterthought said: 'You need towels?'

I felt like I must say yes to something so nodded. Thrusting a bunch in my hands she smiled then began to wheel her trolley away. She stopped.

'Don't leave room,' she added, then she was on her way.

I stood for a full minute, maybe even two, trying to work out what to do next. I felt a little numb, still convinced this wasn't actually happening to me. Then in a complete act of lunacy, I decided not to heed the good advice I'd just seconds ago been given, pulled on some shorts and left my room.

The intensity of the rain hit me immediately. It seemed to be coming from every direction, not just the sky. In fact it was bouncing so hard off the ground that it was actually raining upwards. In less than five seconds I was soaked to the skin and reception was at least a one-minute walk.

Too headstrong to head back I began to run – or at least as close an approximation to a run as you can get when you're in flip-flops on a sopping wet concrete walkway. When I reached the stairs I felt like I was trying to cross a river in spate. Each step neck-breakingly slippery underfoot. I picked my way down, for an instant wondering how I would ever get back up – then dismissing this as I continued on my obstacle course.

If I'd thought the stairs bad I was in for a rude awakening on the patio. With nothing to hold on to I felt my foot lose purchase in my ill-chosen footwear and I skidded forward, giving the skin between my toes what can only be described as the mother of all wedgies. I tried to curse to alleviate the pain but the wind stole my breath before I could finish it. There was nothing else for it – I kicked off my flip-flops and left them there, stranded souls in an increasing sea of water. From here I could see a dim light from the front desk – I had nearly made it. Summoning all my energy I made a dash for it, overestimated how much forward throttle I would need and, as I placed my wet foot on the shiny tiled floor and began to perform the splits against my will, grabbed the arm of a surprised bell boy and wrestled myself up to standing, my legs throbbing as I tried to calmly assert myself to the receptionist.

'I'm wondering when my bus will be here to take me to Havana,' I said, in what I hoped sounded more like the voice of a calm and collected traveller and not an asthmatic who has pushed themselves too hard at the gym.

'No, no bus – stay in your room ma'am,' she replied politely.

'I don't think you understand,' I tried again, 'today I am leaving for Havana.'

'No – no-one is leaving – no bus to Havana today or tomorrow – Rita is coming – Hurricane Rita is coming.'

Finally her words sunk in. I wasn't going to Havana. I wasn't going anywhere, not for at least two days. It was pretty devastating as bad news goes. As if on cue, the rain began to get heavier – as if someone up there was as cut up about the news as I was. The receptionist began to pack up her things and placed a sign on the desk saying that it would now be unmanned and to call a number for information. Things were getting serious.

'You need to stay in your roo…' she shouted as I started my epic journey back to the dry haven of my bed, her last syllable already stolen by the hurricane.

As I slammed the door behind me, I was relieved to be back in safety. After the growing storm outside everything seemed ridiculously still and quiet. I walked over to the bed and felt around on the bedside table for the remote control.

The fuzz of a detuned telly greeted me, its flickering black and white snow loud and unhelpful. I changed the channel – the same. And again, and again – nothing. Eventually I stumbled on a black screen. I left it on and lay back on the bed. I felt cold from the rain and grabbed at the duvet. The sensation of warm sheets was instantly comforting and within minutes, without meaning to, I had drifted off to sleep.

Some hours later, talking stirred me from my empty dreams and I sat bolt upright wondering who had got into my room. The TV channel had now started and a Cuban woman was talking in Spanish, evidently about the impending hurricane. I rubbed my eyes. Try as I might to summon my Year 9 Spanish from high school, I couldn't understand a single word – with the odd exception of the word Rita, thrown in every few sentences. I grabbed the remote again and flicked around. Finally I found the one English channel – an American news station.

But due to tense relations between Cuba and the American Government, despite the fact that the hurricane was clearly en route to hitting land in roughly the spot I was standing, the weather woman refused to acknowledge it. Even as the great red collection of contours clustered together on her map span dangerously close to the Cuban landmass, she failed to mention the Caribbean community by name. I was mesmerised by this complete avoidance of the country in spite of our impending brush with a life-threatening cyclone. I did half wonder why they didn't simply remove Cuba from the map. How infuriating it was to need information and to be denied it. I turned off the TV in disgust.

Only then did I begin to hear the rain on my window. Only now could I hear the screams of someone outside. I watched as the balcony windows on my upstairs apartment shook as though being forced by a persistent intruder determined to get inside. I stood up and walked over to them, instinctively moving my hands towards the handle to check that they were secure. Even in the tiny gap between them I could feel the power of the wind, and water was beginning to seep underneath, creating a pool on the floor.

I looked down and saw a woman screaming at her children to come back in. They'd made a bid for the pool and were now being blown around as though they were made of paper. A resort worker appeared from nowhere, grabbed their hands, and ran them back to their mother. Then he disappeared back towards the reception building. I went to retrieve the towels I'd got from the maid earlier to keep the spreading flood from reaching the bed.

That was the most excitement for the next couple of hours. I went from lying on the bed counting the dots on the ceiling to jumping up and looking out the window to see if anything else had happened. I laboured over making a sandwich with my boiled egg and cheese, spent about fifteen minutes trying to work out just what was in the tiny foil sachets at the bottom of the bag (I went with paprika and salt in the end) and whether or not the cheese spread had garlic in it, and switched on the TV again before bemoaning its lack of pertinent information in English. Momentarily, around midday, it all seemed to die down. The wind wasn't as strong and peering out of my window I spied two lads dashing for the bar. It seemed like a good idea until a member of staff yelled at them to get back in their room as it wasn't over yet.

As if on cue, more rain began to tip down from above, surges of water flooded into the inner courtyard and the clouds billowed as though enraged. Rumbles frequently filled the air as thunder and lightning accompanied the wind and my windows shook violently as I cowered under the safety of my duvet.

I felt my phone vibrate – a text.

HURRICANE IN CUBA – R U OK? came a message from home.

OK, BUT V.V. WINDY I replied.

GET IN THE BATHTUB! was the slightly alarmist advice that came back to me and I turned off the phone. The bathtub was shallow, and the bathroom window was merely slats of glass, easily dislodged – and besides, it was too cold.

Things seemed to reach a crescendo around mid-afternoon, with a roar of wind so loud I momentarily considered saying the Lord's Prayer even though I'm not religious, before quickly quietening down again. By about 5.30 p.m. it seemed brighter and the phone in my room rang. It was the chambermaid telling me that it was safe to come to dinner at 7 p.m.

After changing my outfit a few times to preoccupy my mind from my growing hunger, I made my way down, and watched as other guests cautiously appeared from their rooms. It was still pretty dark and with our evident wish to eat, none of us seemed to take in the aftermath of our brush with Rita.

Over dinner I heard that she was making her way up to Texas or Louisiana – apparently the Cubans didn't reciprocate the Americans' refusal to talk about them. In Havana five inches of rain was said to have fallen and several villages were flooded. We'd missed the eye of the storm by a matter of miles. I went to bed that night wondering what would happen next.

Finally some real daylight brought me out of sleep the next morning. I looked outside to a milky coloured dawn sky. I opened the balcony door and was hit by a wave of humid air – the temperature was already starting to rise. Below my feet, tree branches had broken off and smaller, more fragile palms were doubled over, snapped by the force of the sixty-five miles per hour gusts. Someone had obviously left an inflatable pool toy outside which now sat high up on the roof of the dining hall, deflated and looking sorry for itself.

I pulled on my coat and made my way downstairs. Dirty water still sat on the concrete, pools of it formed at uneven joins of the red paving. The chambermaid was joining other workers picking up debris and trying to brush the standing water into the overflow near the pool or away on to the beach. She looked over at me and, despite all this mess, she smiled.

'Ma'am – ma'am!' I turned around to see the receptionist from the previous day running over to me. 'Good news, your bus to Havana will come tomorrow morning at seven a.m.'

I thanked her but felt odd. Heading off to Havana didn't seem as important now as it had a day ago; neither did the rum that the barman was already pouring for me and the other guests now emerging from their rooms. From across the pool I heard a scream – but this time it was an unmistakable cry of glee. A little girl had just been told that the ice cream dispenser was working again and she could have her treat. How quickly paradise had returned.

I picked up a large palm leaf from the floor. In a way we were all irresponsible to be here now I supposed, but it didn't mean that we had to stay that way. Clasping the stem in my hand, I began to sweep the debris near my feet on to the sand – despite the protest of the barman for me to stop and come and have a drink. For now, the rum could wait.

Phoebe Smith's passion for both writing and travel has taken her on adventures all around the world – from wild camping in Scotland, to climbing 5,000-metre peaks in the Himalayas, tracking polar bears with the Inuit in Nunavik and hunting the Northern Lights in Arctic Norway. She is editor  of *Wanderlust* travel magazine and regularly writes for a number of newspapers and magazines in the UK and overseas. She is currently writing Bradt's *Wilderness Weekends* (due out in March 2015), and is also the author of *Extreme Sleeps: Adventures of a Wild Camper*, *The Camper's Friend* and the Cicerone guide to the *Peddars Way and Norfolk Coast Path*. Follow her latest escapades on Twitter @PhoebeRSmith.

A Narrow Escape

Liam Lambert

The air gauge on my scuba gear read three minutes remaining. My two daughters' gauges read twelve minutes. I was hyperventilating and had to get to the surface, forty feet above... now.

The morning had started beautifully. Mary, my wife, and Sarah, the youngest of our three daughters, decided to sleep in for a few hours while I went scuba diving with our two other daughters, Juliana, twenty-two, and Meghan, twenty-one. We were staying on an idyllic island in the Maldives called Baros. We had been there for a few days; the weather was dreamily warm and balmy, the sea crystal clear and the surrounding rock pools teemed with fish of all colours. A perfect Christmas away from chilly London. Our cabins were only twenty feet from the water's edge. The island, unusually, was surrounded by a manmade, chest-high coral wall fifty metres from the shore, presumably a water break.

Having scuba dived for over three decades, I was confident of my knowledge and ability. Checklists are essential and although the divemaster was expertly qualified I took comfort in running through my own. My daughters are trained in scuba diving and, although not as enthusiastic as me, they usually joined me on a dive.

So we three intrepid divers were up at first light for a 'tide, weather and safety' briefing with the divemaster. The boat had a large open diving platform astern. The air tanks were lashed to the deck. As we manoeuvred away from the pier and out of the small harbour, Juliana brought to my attention something unusual. The tide seemed to be running very rapidly and high; for the first time since we arrived some days ago, the five-foot wall surrounding Baros was almost under water. I foolishly dismissed it as a rising spring tide. We carried on and sped into the cerulean Indian Ocean, oblivious as to what was about to unfold.

The plan that day was a 'drift dive', where the divers enter the water at a particular point and allow the current to sweep them along the reef. The boat drifts along at the same natural pace and one hour later picks up the divers. That was our expectation: an effortless dive along a colourful reef in the exotic archipelago of the Maldives.

How wrong we were! Within minutes of our descent we were at thirty to forty feet, feeling euphoric, weightless, energised and inquisitive. Then, frighteningly, sand and silt from the depths swirled up and around us. The fish became skittish, disappearing into the safety of the coral as if threatened by a predator. I looked about to check and made my way closer to my children, ensuring they were within reach. They were enjoying the changing environment. The current pushed us ever faster as the swirling sand cut visibility. The face of the reef seemed to rush past us as the current gained speed. I lost sight of our divemaster; it was time to take things in to my own hands. I finned to Juliana and grabbed her arm. Now linked tightly we both made our way to Meghan and enveloped her with our arms. She was having a great time turning and tumbling in the rapidly flowing sea. Our divemaster was still nowhere to be seen.

With Dad holding his girls so tightly, they understood something serious was afoot. We held on to each other as we were churned and turned the full length of the reef. At the end the world seemed to reverse itself. The sand and silt changed its pattern and we immediately commenced a return journey back along the reef. Ten minutes later we were back at the point where the dive had started. Again though, almost on cue, the underwater world reversed itself. We were dragged, swirling, clinging on to each other, back along the reef, now bare, grey and fishless. The sea was opaque. My children were alert and concerned but not panicking. I, on the other hand, was in blind terror, hyperventilating, bruised from bashing into the reef and trying to protect my precious diving partners.

My air gauge read three minutes. My children's twelve minutes. Then out of the frightening murk the divemaster appeared. He signed to us that I was to surface immediately. I was to wait on the surface and flag the dive boat. Thankfully it was only metres away.

It was not a spring tide that morning of 26 December 2004. It was a tsunami, which killed 273,000 people across the Indian Ocean. Meghan, Juliana and I survived.

Liam Lambert is an international luxury hotelier who has lived in eleven cities in eight countries, spending many years with Westin Hotels, Mandarin Oriental and Oberoi Hotels. Most of his adventures are shared with his wife, Mary, and their three children. Liam is Irish by birth, internationalist by choice. He is presently reinventing himself as a writer and artist, and this story was an entry to the Bradt/*Independent on Sunday* Travel Writing Competition.

At the Border, Four Months after Gaddafi

Tom Chesshyre

At the Houmt Souk taxi rank all was confusion. Several pot-bellied men wearing jeans appeared to be in charge of proceedings – a team of Fat Controllers, each with the air of 'This is my patch, I regard with disdain anyone who says or thinks otherwise'.

I went up to one of the rank's 'commanders-in-chief', naturally upsetting all the others, who crowded round to listen and have their say. Through a fraught series of questions, charged with a sense of general indignation and competitive bitterness (the bottom line seemed to be that they all wanted me to go in *their* vehicle even if it was not heading in the right direction), I discovered that I should take one of the *louage* (rental) minibuses to the Libyan border.

The minibuses were coloured white, while regular taxis were yellow. The regular taxis were not licensed to go all the way to the Libyan border, though one driver had offered a 'special rate' – just for me – of about US$100. In the end I bought a ticket from a kiosk for about US$3 and went to the appropriate white minibus. The passengers – we numbered four – had to wait until the tally reached seven. This was the profitability tipping point at which the driver would have enough cash to make the journey worthwhile. Without three more, we would be staying in Houmt Souk, Djerba, for the foreseeable future.

And so I found myself on a plastic grey seat with a cigarette burn in a freezing minibus, sitting behind a man wearing a grey tunic with a pointed hood. He had kept the hood up to stay warm. A voice on a radio rattled on importantly, before the station switched to a mournful Arabic tune. Next to the man in the tunic a younger fellow in camouflage trousers was restlessly pecking on a mobile phone. Thanks to him, I had discovered that the bus went as far as the town of Ben Guerdane – not right up to the R'as Ajdir border, as I had imagined. Another taxi was required from Ben Guerdane. But I was too bamboozled by the ticket negotiations for this taxi to worry about the next part of the journey. I settled down awaiting further travellers, while reading a piece in *La Presse Tunisie* about how Tunisia was experiencing the coldest winter for five years and that '*il continue à neiger sur le nord-ouest*'. The temperature was so low it was snowing not so far away.

Passenger Number Seven eventually arrived, and we departed. We crossed sandy scrubland leading to the causeway, where we were waved through with a nonchalant flip of a hand by a soldier wearing shades, and set out across the sun-dazzled, muddy-green water. Flocks of seagulls swept across the seascape, looking like handfuls of confetti. A solid stone fort stood sentinel on the horizon, rising up through the haze.

We reached the mainland and set off through olive groves, the soul-searching Arabic music continuing on the radio. At a little town with houses hidden behind walls topped with jagged pieces of glass, we turned at a junction boasting Pizzeria Hannibal, and then hurtled onwards. We crossed another causeway with a *garde nationale* checkpoint, and I wondered if the dull grey land I could see ahead might be the start of Libya. The landscape was flat and sandy and inhospitable – it felt as though we had come to the end of the earth.

The Ben Guerdane bus station was an unprepossessing, windswept spot. We alighted into a litter-strewn yard, where I found myself in step with the man wearing camouflage trousers. The two of us were ushered to a yellow taxi by various locals, and we were soon sharing a vehicle, heading to the border (at least I hoped so).

I asked my new companion what he had been doing in Djerba. 'Holiday, my friend,' he replied; he was a Libyan taking a break. 'Four or five days. Rest and relaxation.' He was in his late twenties, or so I thought, and had a slightly world-weary air. He spoke as though he was dragging the words from his chest – but was perfectly pleasant.

He asked me where I was going.

I explained that I was about to set off on a trip across Libya. He turned round sharply from the front passenger seat and looked me squarely in the eyes, peering through thin-framed circular glasses. 'Just be careful, my friend,' he said alertly. 'Very careful. There are weapons everywhere in Libya: guns, guns, guns.'

He fixed his gaze long enough to be certain I had got this message, before repeating: 'Guns, my friend.' He wore black leather gloves and was smoking a Marlboro Red cigarette. His hair was long and fashioned in a style that reminded me of Michael Jackson. Yet he seemed to be old beyond his years, speaking like an elderly man reflecting on a long hard life.

He returned to examining his mobile phone, as we passed along a corridor of stalls selling tyres, ceramics, wicker baskets, cuddly camels and 42-inch televisions – they were in cardboard boxes that displayed all the details. Ben Guerdane seemed to be a centre of cross-border commerce… and local tourism, too, if the stuffed camels and other tourist knick-knacks were anything to go by.

As we made our way along a road partially covered with sand drifts and busy with lopsided trucks transporting crates, I asked my companion about Libya since the revolution: he was, after all, the first Libyan I had met and I was curious to get an early report. I was travelling as a 'tourist' and I tried to give this impression – this was to be my cover, how I intended to present myself in Libya. Saying I was a journalist might raise too many questions. I was simply a (very) eccentric tourist, slightly lost and visiting a country to which no international travel company was selling holidays. What was life like since Gaddafi's demise, I asked, taking notes in a manner that I hoped made me seem like an eager visitor with a travel journal. My companion turned slowly again.

'Just two things have changed,' he said calmly and softly. 'The flag and the leader.'

He seemed a little suspicious of me – cautious, sussing me out. He asked where I was from.

'Ah, the British!' he said, his wary attitude disappearing in an instant and his face coming to life. 'The British! We love the British! And the French! You helped us kill Gaddafi!'

He was suddenly full of warmth. He explained that he had thought I was Dutch, German or American. 'I have met Americans: but never a British!' he exclaimed. He swivelled round completely from the front seat and was animated. 'I have longed to meet a British!'

The road had turned in to a sand tunnel; the wind had whipped up and you could hardly see more than twenty metres. My companion told me his name was Sotyn Al-Tekr and that he had fought for the rebels against Gaddafi in Zawiya. He was not in his late twenties. He was just twenty-three and now serving as a sergeant in the army maintaining order while the National Transition Council ran the country in the lead-up to elections due to be held later in the year.

Sotyn brought out his mobile phone and began flicking through images on the monitor. He turned the phone so I could see a picture. It was of him lying on a narrow bed. He had a huge bandage wrapped around his midriff, as though he was halfway through the process of mummification. He was grinning and making a Winston Churchill V-sign.

'For three days I was without doctor,' Sotyn explained. 'It was shrapnel. We were just pistols at the start, sometimes no pistols. Gaddafi had machine guns and tanks.'

The battle for Zawiya, a major oil port fifty kilometres to the west of Tripoli, had been an important part of the struggle that brought about the regime's demise. After Zawiya, Tripoli had fallen. The capture of the capital had marked the practical end for Gaddafi, who hung on in hiding until he was tracked down to the coastal city of Sirte – close to his hometown – and dragged out of a drainage pipe, beaten, attacked with a bayonet and killed on 20 October 2011 (four months before my visit). Nobody is sure exactly what happened – whether Gaddafi was shot dead or not, for example – though it has since come to light in a Human Rights Watch report that sixty-six of his supporters were summarily executed after his capture, almost certainly including his son Mutassim. It was on that day, with the trio of North African revolutions complete, that I had first formulated the idea of my trip from Tunisia to Libya and on to Egypt.

I said to Sotyn that I thought he was very brave.

'I'm brave because I help my people,' he answered plainly, in a manner that suggested that bravery was nothing: the impulse to help in the struggle overrode any decision-making in the matter.

The sandstorm was swirling viciously, the taxi was being buffeted by wind, and we were passing along a section of road surrounded by razor wire. It had become a desolate, bitter day.

'I was a sniper,' said Sotyn. He showed me another picture from his phone, which captured him wearing a balaclava and holding a rifle. He looked terrifying: a killer, an assassin. The picture was the screen saver on his phone. With his camouflage trousers, T-shirt, fleece and Michael Jackson hair, Sotyn could pass for a member of a 1980s funk band, but in the picture he looked deadly.

'I shot at a machine gun used by Gaddafi's men,' he said. 'I got the people. I got them.'

How many did he kill, I asked.

He paused, thinking about this. We were pulling into a yard with a road leading off across the madly sandy world outside. Then Sotyn said quietly,

'Really, I don't count.'

He was subdued, and I realised that somehow that was not the right question to have asked. Perhaps his break in Djerba – which had been a centre for the rebels plotting the downfall of Tripoli – had been to take his mind off what happened in the bloody uprising. As many as thirty thousand died and fifty thousand were wounded in the struggle; no-one knows the figures for certain as there was a media clampdown during the revolution.

The border at R'as Ajdir during a sandstorm is hellish. Sotyn parted after we exchanged mobile phone numbers. He said that he could show me around Misrata, a city that was also the scene of some of the bloodiest battles during the revolution, if I liked. He took another taxi across the border. But as a foreigner I walked up to a booth at the edge of a hangar with a green roof, where a dozen people were waiting.

The winds had intensified into a full-blown gale. It was bitterly cold and horns from vehicles either impatient to leave or to enter Libya were honking almost continuously. I was the only white face. I joined the queue clutching my passport and my 'letter of invitation', which explained that I was coming on business to visit an oil company. Libya required such a document. There were no tourist visas; instead I had to collect a business visa-on-arrival. The local tour company I had contacted in Tripoli had suggested that this subterfuge was the best way of getting into the country. I was their first tourist since the revolution. It was all a bit confusing. I knew as much about the Libyan oil industry as I did about the history of nomadic tribes in Mongolia (nothing whatsoever). I was hoping that despite the obvious oddity of the paperwork and my total ignorance, I'd be let in. Everything regarding Libya seemed so chaotic and upside-down since the revolution that I was crossing my fingers that a bit of chaos regarding my visa would fit right in.

A Tunisian in a blue uniform barked 'Passport!' from behind a filthy window. I handed over my passport and the letter. The official perused the documents, and slapped them to one side. He said a word that sounded very much like: 'Baloney!'

Another official appeared and took me to one side. He was short, rotund and had black curly hair that was so oily it appeared glued to his skull. 'What is this?' he said. 'We do not recognise this stamp.' He was pointing to a stamp on the letter of invitation.

I explained that it came from the embassy. He disappeared with my passport and letter.

I waited for an hour. There was no cover and I was quickly coated in sand. At one point Sotyn appeared. His taxi had made it to the front of the long, horn-blasting queue. He argued my case with the oily official, who once again shook his head. On the request of another immigration officer, I called my guide on the other side of the border to try to prove I had a Libyan contact, but his phone was not working (I later learnt the number I'd been given was typed with a digit out of place). I said there was trouble with the phones. 'That is your problem,' he replied, taking my passport away again.

I waited for another hour, at the end of which a tall man with a moustache wearing a trilby and a long black coat approached. He did not seem to be a regular official. He looked like an archetypal foreign spy out of a James Bond film. He sidled up to me. He had a suggestion. 'Perhaps,' he said, clearing his throat slightly. 'Perhaps, they would like something.'

The penny dropped. 'You mean some money?' I asked.

'Perhaps, perhaps,' he said enigmatically.

'How much should I give?' I enquired.

'How much have you got?' he replied sharply.

I showed him 60 Tunisian dinars (about £24). 'I could give them this, it's all I have,' I said, referring to what I had left of Tunisian cash.

He found this amusing. 'And so go into Libya with no money?' he asked rhetorically. He chuckled to himself. He looked at me in a way that seemed to assess my worth.

'Could you make the suggestion on my behalf?'

'I could do that for you,' he answered discreetly, his eyes twinkling under his trilby.

He disappeared and ten minutes later a man wearing a grubby grey hooded tunic arrived. 'Are you a journalist?' he asked abruptly.

'Yes,' I replied, deciding that honesty was probably the best course of action by that stage – swiftly abandoning my plan to say I was travelling as a tourist. It was my first lesson in interrogation in North Africa (and my first realisation that I would never have cut it as a spy).

'It says here that you are an office manager,' he commented.

'I help to manage an office in which journalists work,' I said carefully, trying to twist my way out of my slight 'lie'.

He made me follow him to another grimy kiosk. I heard a reassuring thud of a stamp. He whispered the word *baksheesh*, and I gave him my dinars. He handed back my passport and letter, and I walked through the whistling wind past a sign that said 'LA TUNISIE VOUS SOUHAITE BON VOYAGE' (Tunisia wishes you a good journey), across a no-man's-land to another sign that needed no translation: 'LIBYA FREE!' Soldiers in khaki were standing by a wall. 'Nationality?' they asked, and seemed delighted by my response. 'Very good!' they said, as though I had personally flown the NATO planes that helped drive back Gaddafi's troops. I kept going along an empty pavement in the direction of yet more immigration kiosks, the ones I needed to pass to get into Libya, but before I reached them a voice called over to me.

It was – by some minor miracle – Othman al-Ghareeb, my fixer for the trip from the west to the east of Libya. 'I wasn't sure you were going to make it,' he said. He was bald, over six feet, wore aviator shades and a shiny black bomber jacket. He had a solid build and was in his thirties. He looked like the right sort of person to sort things out in post-revolutionary Libya. He took me across a sandy yard where lorries stood piled with terracotta tiles. We traversed a wasteland of weeds, went through what seemed to be a gap in a fence and arrived at a single-storey building with broken windows and a door clanging violently against its frame in the fierce wind. He gave my passport to an official; we appeared to have bypassed the regular kiosks, which might have explained the extra 'passport fee' I'd paid in advance in London. We sat on a crumbling wall under a rattling carob tree and next to a pile of old cans, waiting for the official. The passport was returned, fully stamped. We walked out of the border compound to Othman's car.

Through a hole in a fence via a fistful of dinars, I had made it into post-revolutionary Libya – I was a tourist in a land run by rebels with *guns, guns, guns*.

I was also about to enter a capital city where these guns were being fired every night. Within a couple of hours the 'happy shooters' of Tripoli were at it; the hollow tap, tap, tap of bullets echoing in the evening air.

Tom Chesshyre is the author of *A Tourist in the Arab Spring*, published by Bradt, and three previous books: *Tales from the Fast Trains*, shortlisted in the 2012 British Travel Press Awards, *To Hull and Back* and *How Low Can You Go?* He is staff travel writer for *The Times*, where he has worked since 1997. He lives in London.

Intrigue Under the Big Screen
Rolf Potts

From the moment I enter the cinema and start searching in the dark for a seat, I can tell something is not quite right.

For starters, the movie on the big screen isn't *Die Hard*, as I had expected, but a black and white seventies-era Arabic film starring a polyester-clad protagonist with sideburns the size of brillo pads. I go back out to the foyer to enquire about *Die Hard*, but the doorman just waves me back inside. Figuring a little patience and curiosity can't hurt, I find a seat near the aisle and try to make sense of the film.

The plot proves to be a mesmerisingly bad mix of action, romance, mystery, slapstick comedy and social commentary. So broad is the premise that the hero seems to spend most of his time racing from genre to genre. In the span of a few minutes, we see him running down the street shooting a gun, breaking up a squabble between his enormously fat neighbour and her improbably skinny husband, making an emotional phone call to a worried-looking woman, and sitting in jail while his cellmate dreams of belly dancers. The token sex scene – no more than thirty seconds from foreplay to cigarette – features no disrobing, no stylised fadeaways and no changes in facial expression. After a while, I can't help enjoying it.

Then, just as the bad guys are celebrating their apparent triumph – just as the fat neighbour lady accidentally uncovers a clue that will change everything – the reels change, and an old Hong Kong action scene flickers on to the screen.

I wait for the Jordanians in the audience to whistle, throw popcorn or shout curses at the projectionist. Instead, nothing happens. Small groups of Arab men slouch in their seats, chatting and smoking cigarettes; others get up and make their way to the bathroom under the stage. A few fellows stand up from their seats to stretch their legs, but not a soul expresses any discontent.

After about ten minutes, the Hong Kong movie ends and the lights come up. A couple of vendors stroll into the theatre to sell sandwiches and tea. Figuring this to be some sort of timeout while the projectionist searches for the last reel of the Arabic movie, I stay in my seat.

When the lights go down again, however, a blurry, French soft-porn movie comes up on the screen – again without a peep of protest.

As intrigued as ever, I settle into my plywood theatre seat and wait.

When I first arrived in Amman from the ancient stone city of Petra that morning, I knew that I wouldn't devote much of my time to standard tourism in Jordan's capital. Granted, the city has a long and storied history – both King David and King Nebuchadnezzar II sacked the place long ago – but its modern incarnation just doesn't have much character when compared with other regional capitals such as Cairo or Damascus.

Rather, with tidy concrete buildings on its myriad hillsides and late-model Nissans navigating its calm streets, Amman struck me more as a bedroom community than a place to explore. And since Petra had already given me my fill of ancient monuments, I decided to forgo the smattering of ruins in Amman. Instead, I sought out what the city had to offer in the way of Hollywood-style entertainment.

Admittedly, watching American movies while visiting foreign countries is a bit contradictory, but it's actually one of my favourite travel vices. This is because travel – which is commonly seen as an escape from the routines of home – can often take on a routine of its own through simple, recurring challenges like communication, transportation and nutrition. Even within the escapist setting of travel, I've found that movies allow me to enter into a neutral territory – a darkened, womblike zone where, for a couple of hours, all reality is suspended and I can let my imagination be painted with glorious, nonsensical shades of possibility. I find that I leave the cinema with a heightened sense of magic. When I walk outside, the foreign streets have become even more vivid and intimate than they were before.

Granted, it doesn't change my life or enlarge my brain, but the visceral buzz is worth the admission fee.

In Amman, recent Hollywood movies are screened in the shopping malls of upscale neighbourhoods such as Shmeisani, and cost about the same as they would in America. Older American and Arabic movies, on the other hand, play in the rundown cinemas of the downtown area, and cost just 1 dinar (US$1.43). Since my hotel was downtown, I decided to see what these cheaper cinemas had to offer. When I saw a poster for the 1988 Bruce Willis action flick hanging outside a small cinema on Basman Street, I couldn't resist.

Twenty minutes into the French porno, however, I am beginning to question the wisdom of my decision. By anyone's standards, most soft-porn movies are lacking in narrative cohesiveness, but when the actual sex scenes are edited out, as they are in Jordan, the result is almost incomprehensible, like reading a comic book with no pictures: all the BOOM!s and POW!s of the plot seem downright moronic when you can't actually see the fight.

I'm pretty sure this particular movie is about a man with a moustache who woos a woman pharmacist in an effort to seduce her daughter – but I can't be sure. The various reels look as if they've been played every day for the past ten years; all the colours have washed out into shades of brown, red or orange and some scenes have no audio whatsoever.

I suppose I could just get up and walk out of the cinema, but a dull sense of irony keeps me glued to my seat. Watching French porno in Jordan has a certain low-culture appeal; it's as incongruent as watching a Farsi-dubbed episode of '*CHiPs*' in Iran or meeting a villager in rural Cambodia who claims to be a big Ron Jeremy fan. There must be a future cocktail party anecdote in here somewhere.

I don't have to wait long, however, before my assumptions are trumped.

At some point after the third missing sex scene, a hefty Jordanian man settles into the seat next to mine. He sits so close that I move one seat over just to give us both a bit of breathing room. After five minutes, he leans over toward me.

'*Toilette?*' he says.

I gesture to the place under the stage where all the men have been coming and going since the first feature. '*Henek,*' I say. 'Over there.'

Toilette Man waddles off to the bathroom, and I return to the befuddling tale of the moustache man and the pharmacist.

Five minutes later, Toilette Man returns and sits right next to me. '*Toilette!*' he exclaims, looking somewhat irritated.

I give him a puzzled look. '*Mafeesh mushkellah,*' I tell him, patting my bladder. 'No problem.'

Toilette Man gives me a leering grin, then gently slips his hand on to the place where my thigh meets my hip.

His grope sends me springing toward the ceiling. I make it up to a high crouch before I bang my knees on the seats in front of me and collapse back into my chair. Toilette Man looks over at me, embarrassed; I hear tittering behind me. Flustered, I retreat to an empty corner of the cinema and wait to see what happens next.

Since the men behind me saw what happened – and since, for all its modernity, Jordan is a very conservative society – I expect Toilette Man to flee the cinema in shame. Instead, he just moves up a couple of rows and begins to stroke the hair of a boy in a leather jacket.

Up on the screen, the moustache man is forcing the pharmacist to perform a late-night striptease in front of her apothecary; below, in the seats, Leather Jacket Boy leans over and gently rests his head on Toilette Man's shoulder.

A few moments later, the French porno stops and the theatre lights come on. The film had been playing for only fifty minutes when it was interrupted, but as usual there is no reaction from the audience. As the tea vendors file in from outside, I take a good look at the other men in the cinema. Only then does it dawn on me why they haven't been paying any attention to the film: they're all paying attention, with various levels of erotic enthusiasm, to each other. But strangely, none of them 'looks' gay.

It occurs to me that what I've stumbled into under the Jordanian big screen is a kind of sexual middle ground unique to deeply conservative societies: a symptom not of pure homosexuality per se but the lack of more accessible sexual options for single men in this culture. Granted, the capital looks progressive on the surface, but Jordan is still a society where men who kill their sisters for moral 'honour' receive a reduced prison sentence if they can prove she was promiscuous. Since this makes it prohibitively dangerous for would-be party girls to exercise their sexual freedom, it would appear that a few of the lonely party boys have turned to each other in the darkness of this cinema.

As the lights go down again, I get one last surprise: the final movie of the evening is not *Die Hard* but *Hard to Kill*, starring Steven Seagal. As the opening scenes flicker on to the screen, I get up to go – not because I particularly dislike Seagal or fear more homoerotic come-ons but because I've lost all faith in the projectionist's ability to show an entire movie.

Reasoning that I've already gotten my dinar's worth of entertainment in this place, I walk out to Basman Street and hail a cab, hoping to catch a late movie in the more predictable confines of the Shmeisani suburbs.

Rolf Potts has reported from more than sixty countries for the likes of *National Geographic Traveler*, *The New Yorker*, *The Guardian*, *Outside*, *Sports Illustrated* and the Travel Channel. His adventures have taken him across six continents, and include piloting a fishing boat 900 miles down the Laotian Mekong, hitchhiking across Eastern Europe,  traversing Israel on foot, bicycling across Burma, driving a Land Rover across South America, and travelling around the world for six weeks with no luggage or bags of any kind. He is the author of two travel books, *Vagabonding* and *Marco Polo Didn't Go There*.

Scary Biker
Polly Evans

I hadn't told the whole story to Ian and John Fitzwater, the brothers who owned the motorbike rental company. There was something about the way their website proclaimed, 'We are fiercely proud of our range of bikes which are in as-new, showroom condition' which stopped me letting on that the day I picked up the gleaming Suzuki Freewind from their Auckland depot was the first day I had ridden a motorbike without L plates. It was the first day I'd ridden a motorbike without an instructor in tow. And it was the first day I'd ridden a motorbike anything like this big.

Until that day, my trip had seemed a great idea. I was going to spend ten weeks motorcycling round New Zealand, hunting out that endangered species, the Real Kiwi Bloke (who can turn his hand to anything with the aid of a bit of number 8 wire – you know the type), and writing a book about my adventures. In my brand-new, body-hugging motorcycle leathers I'd vroom from the tip of the country at the Bay of Islands with its golden-sand beaches and soaring kauri forests, down past the bubbling geothermal mud pools at Rotorua and over the Cook Strait to South Island with its glacier-tipped Alps and windswept West Coast. I'd try my hand at trout fishing on Lake Taupo, kayak with dolphins at dawn on Milford Sound, and search for kiwis in the dead of night on Stewart Island. I'd spend a day with a bloke in a cow shed and a night in a hut with a team of sheep shearers. It would be winter back home and summer down under. What was not to like?

A man called Paul wheeled my bike out into the forecourt. The bit he parked it on looked precariously sloping. I thought I'd push it to a flatter piece of tarmac a few metres away. I found I couldn't wheel the bike. It was too heavy. A sickly uneasiness spread from my stomach and, beneath my leathers, I began to perspire.

'Can I help you with that?' asked Paul. (New Zealanders are almost pathologically predisposed to be helpful.)

'Thanks,' I squeaked, trying not to sound anxious. Playing for time, I very slowly loaded my luggage into the panniers. I thought a few things might fit in better another way, so I packed them again. And then there was nothing left for me to do. I had no choice but to leave.

'See ya,' Paul chirruped breezily. He seemed entirely aware of the lunacy in which he was complicit.

'See ya,' I squawked like a half-strangled budgerigar.

This bike was huge. Six hundred and fifty ccs hadn't sounded all that large when I'd been back home looking at pictures of bikes on my computer screen and dreaming of roaring down the open road. Six hundred and fifty ccs was terrifying in the flesh. It was only now that it occurred to me that people actually die when riding motorbikes. Never mind the endangerment of the Real Kiwi Bloke – I was well on the way to making myself extinct. And what if I wiped out innocent bystanders to boot? My fantasy was fast disintegrating. As I inched down the tiny hill that led out on to the main road, my self-image plummeted. Gone was the free-as-the-wind leather-clad biker chick. A horribly irresponsible incompetent had slithered sweatily into her place. Gingerly, I turned the throttle. The bike let out a man-eating roar.

I was heading that day to Paihia in the Bay of Islands at New Zealand's northernmost tip. This was where, in 1835, Charles Darwin first stepped foot on New Zealand soil during his voyage on the *Beagle*. New Zealand 'is not a pleasant place,' he wrote in his journal. 'Amongst the natives there is absent that charming simplicity which is found in Tahiti; and the greater part of the English are the very refuse of society.'

Paihia was only a couple of hundred kilometres away – an easy distance for the first day on the road, and after about twenty minutes or so, I had to admit that things seemed to be going pretty well. I may only have passed my motorcycle test three weeks previously but the bike was purring along without a care in the world. More confident now, I looked at the dashboard. That big number in the middle had to be the speed – a rather impressive seventy-five kilometres per hour, I thought. Those little notches down the side must be the petrol except that – hold on a moment – there didn't seem to be any fuel in the tank. There must be fuel, I told myself. After all, the bike was moving. I looked again, more closely now, and then I saw it: right at the bottom, in the red 'empty' segment, three little notches turned to two. There was nothing for it. I was going to have to stop.

I'd just passed a town called Warkworth. I successfully executed a U-turn and turned off the main road into a petrol station. Without a hitch, I filled the tank. Too smugly, I left the petrol station. A traffic light turned red. I braked, forgetting to use the clutch. The bike bunny-hopped and crashed to the ground.

I had no hope of picking it up. It was far too heavy. Half an hour ago, I hadn't managed to wheel it upright across a few inches of forecourt. I pretended to try, if only to placate the drivers in the queue behind me. They beeped their horns.

'Can I help you with that?' A woman appeared laden with grocery bags. I knew that, even between the two of us, we'd never lift the bike but a humiliation shared is a humiliation halved so I eagerly accepted her offer. She put down her bags and we hauled and we heaved and we humphed. And then, as if by magic, the bike rose from the ground. Behind me stood a massive Maori man, whose tattooed biceps bulged from his singlet. He appeared to have lifted the bike with a single, muscle-bound finger.

'Oh, gosh, thank you,' I stuttered, 'You see, I've only just picked it up from the hire shop, I've never ridden it before…'

The big bloke grinned. I braced myself. I was sure he was about to say something horribly derisory.

'Nice bike,' he said. And then, still smiling, he strolled into the middle of the road, stopped the traffic, and waved me on my way.

Polly Evans is the author of *Yukon: The Bradt Travel Guide* (winner of the British Guild of Travel Writers' award for Best Guidebook) and Bradt's *Northern Lights,* as well as five travel narrative books: *It's Not About the Tapas, Kiwis Might Fly* (which tells the full story of her motorbiking  escapades Down Under), *Fried Eggs with Chopsticks, On a Hoof and a Prayer* and *Mad Dogs and an Englishwoman.* She writes regularly for national newspapers and travel magazines, while her BBC radio documentary, *The Other Guantánamo,* won the British Guild of Travel Writers' Best Travel Broadcast award. www.pollyevans.com

An Incident on the Road
Stuart Forster

May isn't the best month to explore southern India. Temperatures and humidity run high ahead of the monsoon. Rather than postcard-perfect blue, the skies of Kerala are often a drab grey, making for flat photos that do nothing positive for the otherwise eye-catching landscapes, beaches and temples of this part of the world. Unsurprisingly, I hadn't run into many foreign tourists over the past few days.

I was heading south while undertaking research for a book on driving holidays in India. The print deadline meant I couldn't wait until October or November, which are ideal for seeing the palm-rich state at its verdant best. Visiting during the monsoon season, which tends to roll in at the start of June, would be sheer folly. Sections of road are susceptible to flooding and even the most industrious of windscreen wipers struggle to clear the prodigious volume of water dumped during downpours, making driving nigh on impossible.

Even in good weather, driving on Indian roads can be a challenge. Urban areas are prone to frustrating snarl-ups as drivers weave for position across the full breadth of streets. The tooting and parping of auto rickshaw and car horns is more or less incessant while vehicles jockey haltingly for progress. I've travelled on road surfaces that are so riddled with pot-holes that they've reminded me of lunar maps. Buses and trucks barrel along assuming right of way based on size alone, blowing their super-charged horns as a warning that they're overtaking. They bear handwritten signs – such as 'horn please' with a depiction of an old-fashioned, squeezable bugle-like horn – inviting other drivers to blow their horns as a warning that they are about to drive past. There's no getting away from the fact that, at times, Indian roads are bone-shaking, nerve-jangling places to travel.

Sensibly, the publisher had insisted that I use a professional driver, and recommended a guy named Srinivas, a slight, moustachioed man in his twenties. I'd been commissioned to write about the drive between Mangalore, in Karnataka, and Kanyakumari, the most southerly point of the subcontinent, in Tamil Nadu. In addition to his driving ability I was told Srinivas would be ideal because he had a good track record while out on research trips and spoke Kannada, Malayalam and Tamil; of course he spoke English too, and a smattering of Hindi. He was likable, and after almost a week sitting next to each other we were getting on well. His driving was safe, he was easy to chat to and, importantly, I had the gut feeling that he was honest and reliable. Living in India for four years had taught me much about the value of listening to intuition.

I was looking forward to exploring the sites that we'd pass along our route. These included old forts, temples and mosques; places such as the red laterite-built Bekal Fort, overlooking the Arabian Sea, and Thalassery – previously known as Tellicherry – home to one of the oldest cricket grounds in the country. Despite having a wealth of heritage, vast swathes of India were only gradually waking up to the value of embracing domestic tourism among the rapidly expanding demographic group with rupees to spend on leisure and travel. Quite a few of the places we visited had little or no information about them on the internet and next to nothing in guidebooks. It was proving a real pleasure to get off the beaten track and see more than merely the luxury *kettuvallam* (house boats) and Ayurvedic resorts for which Kerala is renowned abroad. I'd walked on Kappad Beach, where Vasco da Gama landed back in 1498, and felt a genuine sense of adventure in making this trip.

The budget was tight. We were eating well – I love the aromatic, coconut-rich cuisine of Kerala – though we were by no means heading to fancy restaurants. We were overnighting in guesthouses and motels. They were simple places but perfectly adequate; I was sleeping well after our busy days of travel, research and note-taking.

On the outskirts of Alappuzha, the city also known as Alleppey, we'd spent the night in a quiet motel. Starting out early the next morning, I greeted Srinivas and climbed into the car, parked where we'd left it the night before in the safety of the gated courtyard. We made our way towards the national highway then closed our windows and cranked up the AC, as Srinivas called the air conditioning, with the goal of spending the night at Varkala Beach.

We'd been on the road at least an hour. The highway only has one lane in each direction for most of its route. We were zipping past men wearing white dhotis, cotton wrapped around their waists and folded well above their knees so that they could pedal their old-fashioned looking metal-framed bicycles at a steady but leisurely pace. Settlements weren't concentrated in this region; they stretched out along the highway. I welcomed the gaps between buildings as a chance to see greenery, usually palm groves, and enjoyed our stop at one of the many ramshackle tea stalls for a glass of sweet, milky, spice-infused chai. We'd driven past I don't know how many shops selling mobile phonecards, biscuits in glass jars, ribbons of little foil-sealed sachets of chewable seeds and bananas hanging in bunches. People seemed to be forever milling along the roadside and chatting in front of shops.

I was lost in idle observation, when Srinivas shifted in his seat a little to take a better look in the rear-view mirror. He had a quizzical expression and his eyes kept darting back to the mirror from the road.

'What's up?' I asked.

'I don't know, Sir. The driver behind is being erratic,' he answered, concerned but not overly so. 'He is very close to us.'

I looked round and a beige Austin Ambassador, that stalwart of the subcontinent's roads, was tailgating us while veering hard from side to side, reminding me of the movement racing drivers sometimes make before roaring forward on an overtaking manoeuvre.

'What an idiot,' I commented; curses and swear words have much more impact and shock value in India than in my native city of Sunderland. 'Why doesn't he just overtake us?'

In a short while a gap opened in the oncoming traffic and, sure enough, the Ambassador started to accelerate past. The two chubby occupants of the car eyeballed us as they drew alongside. They were in their forties, I guessed, had moustaches and brushed-back bouffant-like hairstyles; a look clearly inspired by some movie star or other. I didn't like the look of them but resisted the temptation to flash them a gesture.

I was anticipating that they'd drive by then pull in ahead of us. That wasn't what happened. They pulled across us and braked, in what I read as a move of reckless stupidity. Had it not been for Srinivas's slick response, we would have ploughed into their left-side panelling.

I'm not sure what language he used as the gravel of the unsealed hard shoulder smacked and rattled against the underside of our wheel arches. I guessed from the tone it was his native Kannada and that he was uttering something unsavoury about the driver of the Ambassador. We'd kicked up a cloud of whirling greyish dust. Fortunately the incident had occurred in one of the gaps between shops. If it had taken place a couple of minutes earlier, cyclists or women walking by the roadside may well have been maimed or even killed.

'What on earth was he thinking?' I asked, agitated, while turning to keep my eyes on the car we'd just undertaken in order to avoid a collision.

Srinivas merely shook his head in confusion and concern and pulled back on to the road. 'I don't know, Sir, this driver, he is very bad,' he answered, clearly shaken.

'Well done,' I said encouragingly, 'you did well to avoid an accident there.'

Srinivas didn't answer. His eyes flicked between the mirror and the highway ahead. From the shocked look on his face I knew something was wrong. 'Sir, look,' he said.

The Ambassador was gunning it down the centre of the road, gaining on us. Hopefully this time they'd simply pass on by and be gone. Something told me, though, that we had a problem.

This time the occupants of the beige motor were mouthing in our direction and wafting their arms about in agitation, as if to tell us to get off the road.

'What do they want?' I asked. There seemed little sense in pulling over.

'I don't know, Sir. This is not good. They are bad men,' said Srinivas.

I flicked my hand forward, as if I was trying to swat away an annoying fly, in a gesture signifying they should simply get on with their journey. The man on the nearside was glowering at us.

They pulled ahead and then, without warning, swung across us. It was the type of stop-the-criminal manoeuvre I'd only ever seen made by cop cars in American movies. It was more dramatic, more malevolent than their first effort.

I'm not exactly sure how we avoided hitting them. It was all too quick. All I know is that Srinivas pulled left, I lurched right and we ended up on the gravel again, this time at a stop. The Ambassador pulled in ahead of us, five metres in front.

Before I knew it, the two guys had opened their doors and were coming towards us. This problem wasn't going to go away. They'd tried to run us off the road twice, so I decided we had to confront them. By that, I don't use 'confront them' as a euphemism for getting out and giving them a good pasting, even though I was mightily irked.

I remember looking Srinivas in the eyes and reaching for the door. We nodded at each other and then sprang out. We walked briskly towards the moustachioed men, who were berating us in lilting Malayalam. Srinivas was firing words back, though I had no idea what he was saying. The men were clearly angry, but by now, so were we.

The two men grabbed at Srinivas's arms and pulled him towards their car. This was getting out of control. You can take the boy out of Sunderland but not Sunderland out of the boy; I saw no option but to intervene physically. I surged forward and placed a hand on each of the two malefactors' chests. My sixteen stones of weight helped push them against the boot of their vehicle and free Srinivas from their grasp.

'Get back to the car,' I told Srinivas, 'let's get out of here. Keep your hands off my driver,' I snapped at the two would-be film stars.

'Don't shout at me,' one of them answered back. 'Why you do this?'

'If you try to run us off the road then attack my driver, what do you expect?' I asked, trying to remain calm and de-escalate the situation.

Cars had pulled up alongside us and a bus had by now stopped in the opposite lane. The passengers were gawping at us out of the open windows. I saw one man dismounting from his bicycle. The Ambassador's passenger was clearly telling anyone who'd listen that we were in the wrong. He was whipping himself up into an oratory frenzy of gestures and I sensed the gathering crowd feeding on his anger.

We'd only been at the roadside a matter of seconds but people were amassing and turning into a mob. There must have been twenty to thirty people. I made my way to my side of the car and a group followed me. Others grabbed Srinivas and pushed him against the door. Things were starting to get rough. A couple of men started to rock the car and others joined in; it looked like they were trying to flip it. There was no point in trying to get back in.

'Leave him alone,' I asked, as calmly as I could to those manhandling Srinivas.

I turned and one of the men who'd joined the mob took a step towards me. I recognised the 'I'm not going to back down' look in his eye from the times I'd been involved in rugby pitch punch ups. He was up for doing me a bit of damage. He was a couple of inches shorter than me but I could tell by his athletic build and well-defined arms that he was accustomed to regular physical work.

There was no point in getting physical. Even if I took him down I'd be pounced on by the others. As things looked, they were about to grab me anyway. I'd heard tales and read reports of lynchings and mob justice. The hostile expressions of the men around me had me fearing for my life. I reckoned I was seconds away from being attacked.

I pulled my mobile phone from my pocket with a view to calling the police. My hand was trembling so violently that I couldn't even punch in the code to unlock it and make a call.

I looked back up and the athletic ringleader of the group was within arm's reach, about to make a move.

Then two men started shouting from Srinivas's side of the car. They were not part of the mob, standing a couple of metres further back. They spoke with authority and, whatever they were saying, it was having an effect. The men holding Srinivas let go of him and the tension began to dissipate from the shoulders of the men around me. To this day, I don't know who those two men were.

'Get in your car and go,' said one of them to me.

'What's happening?' I asked, confused, relieved but still shaking.

'Don't ask questions. You must go now. Go!' he intoned the last word in such a way that it was clear we were still in danger and had to get away quickly, before things turned again.

I looked up while getting into the car and saw the two men from the Ambassador watching.

People stood aside and we headed back on to the road. We drove in silence for minutes before either of us spoke.

'What was all that about?' I asked.

'He said we had damaged his car and he wanted money,' answered Srinivas.

'What?' I asked incredulously. 'When?'

'This morning.'

Maybe they had us confused with another vehicle with Karnataka number plates; or perhaps they thought, as a foreigner, I'd be an easy mark.

Our mood was flat. I felt sapped of energy. 'Are you okay, Srinivas?'

'Sir, they are bad men. I am happy that we are here,' he said, sounding anything but happy.

'Let's get to Kollam, find a hotel, and we'll take the day off,' I suggested, after consulting the map. We were shaken but alive. Perhaps being in a city would give us safety if they came looking for us.

'Yes, Sir,' agreed Srinivas.

Aware that we'd just escaped from a life-threatening situation that had, in all, lasted less than two minutes, we drove on, barely speaking.

Stuart Forster is a freelance travel writer and photographer, originally from Sunderland in the northeast of England, who spent five years based in India. He loves being out on the road, undertaking research and capturing images relating to themes such as wildlife, cuisine and culture. The incident described above took place while researching *Driving Holidays Across India,* a travel book which won India's national award for excellence in publishing.

Lost in the USSR

Janice Booth

*T*he narrow riverside track snaked through wiry, ankle-height vegetation which I could feel with my feet but – in the darkness – couldn't see. A yard or so to my left the river raced by, occasional flecks of foam showing creamy against the black. I shuffled forward blindly, trying not to stray towards the water – when suddenly, ahead of me, I heard a rustle of approaching movement...

It was the early spring of 1985: Gorbachev barely settled in power, no stirrings yet of glasnost or perestroika in the Soviet Union, and tourism still in the iron grip of Intourist. To escape its clutches I'd booked two short group trips with a three-day gap between the end of one and the start of the next, allowing me seventy-two hours alone in Moscow. I planned some gentle solo exploration.

On arrival at Sheremetyevo airport – grey, grim and unsmilingly functional – I and the rest of the group were piled into buses and whisked along broad streets to the tourist 'must-sees': Red Square, multi-coloured St Basil's Cathedral, guards goose-stepping solemnly by Lenin's tomb, immense Kremlin walls, huge statues, towering buildings – everything so big and so impersonal. I longed to stroll in narrower streets alongside Moscow's people and to see smaller, older buildings, closer to the heartbeat of this intriguing city. Next day came the museums, art galleries and more imposing architecture; our coach's windows steamed up continuously and misted over, as did our minds. We ate 'traditional Russian meals' in cavernous restaurants and tried to react intelligently to our guide's flood of information, but it was too much, too fast.

Finally the tour ended and the others went home. Relief! I stayed on in the same hotel, the massive Cosmos, its marbled foyer reminiscent of New York's Grand Central Station. The characterless bedrooms stretched along equally characterless corridors, guarded by formidable 'key ladies'. That night the TV in the room next to mine was blaring at full blast and I mimed to the elderly wardress on duty that I couldn't sleep. She waddled fiercely down the corridor and gave the occupant hell, we did a mutual mime of how disgraceful his behaviour was – and she allowed herself a small conspiratorial smile. My first human contact!

At breakfast next morning (blinis and sour cream – bliss) two men in cheap dark suits with padded shoulders studied me from a distance and muttered together. For exploring Moscow I'd brought plain frumpy clothes which I hoped wouldn't distinguish me as a tourist, but my prematurely white hair proved awkward; apparently Muscovite women my age (forty-six) went raven black or improbable chestnut rather than grey. There was a wariness towards Westerners at the time, so I completed my 'disguise' with a headscarf to ward off the furtive stares.

I could just about read the Cyrillic alphabet, useful for deciphering the names of streets and metro stations, but my knowledge of Russian was limited to *yes*, *no*, *please*, *thank you*, *water* and (surprisingly, since I never wanted any) *ice cream*. So, optimistically but somewhat underprepared, I launched myself into Moscow.

For the first day I just walked, following small streets off the tourist routes and looking at older, shabbier architecture which – for me – had far more charm. With their crumbling carvings, patched plaster and fading paint, these were buildings that had been loved. Several small shops were closed, with a notice in the window saying *remont* (repair/refurbishment). There was even a Remont shop closed for remont. Passers-by resembled chunky little parcels, bundled up in their shapeless winter coats. Faces were serious, sad even. This was a tough time for the average Russian, with low salaries and little in the shops. The much-vaunted department store Gum hadn't much on its shelves other than cheap undesirable fashions and various imported toiletries and household goods.

Standing alone in Red Square surrounded by so much history was surprisingly moving. As I watched Muscovites hurrying by, shoulders hunched against the cold, I thought – how amazing to live here and be part of this every day. But then, I felt the same about my favourite bits of London.

Tucked away in a side street, the door of a small onion-domed church was invitingly open. Inside, it glittered with gilt and silver and the rich colours of innumerable icons. The government paid lip service to freedom of religion but in fact only 'official' churches like this one were allowed – others had been forcibly closed and often damaged or left to rot, so those that survived were immensely precious to their congregations. Believers were persecuted at this time, often on the flimsiest of pretexts, and some Christians had been sentenced to years of hardship in labour camps for such 'crimes' as distributing religious literature or speaking against the restrictions. The knowledge of this seemed incongruous as I leant against the wall, enjoying the atmosphere of reverence and faith. An old woman in a faded flowery overall (she'd been cleaning) approached and smiled welcomingly, her eyes speedwell-blue in a weathered face. I gestured that it was a beautiful, peaceful church; she tried, by pointing to numbers on my watch, to tell me when there would be a service. As I left she stroked my arm, urging me to return; she loved the church and wanted me to see it at its best, when it was full of people.

Of course a ticket for the Bolshoi Ballet was a must. The scarlet-coated rep in the Intourist office, her over-plucked eyebrows as unnatural as her jet-black hair, clearly hadn't much time for tourists, but thawed slightly when I said how excited I was to go to such a famous and beautiful theatre. On checking my ticket I found her starchiness had been deceptive: she'd seated me in the front row. The performance – a miscellany of extracts from different ballets – was wonderful, but from close up I could see how patched and threadbare the costumes were. Hard times.

Despite my lack of language, I was getting the feel of the city – and apparently looking sufficiently like a Muscovite: as I left the hotel next morning the doorman challenged me, not realising I was a guest. Later, at the ticket machine in a metro station, a girl of about twelve trustingly held out a coin; I guessed she was asking me if I would change it into smaller ones so she could buy her ticket. I counted them out, and she thanked me politely.

Now I began riding the metro, stopping *en route* to admire the magnificently decorated stations: some Art Deco, some Baroque, some palatial with chandeliers, some with mosaics or stained glass. Twice I rode to the outskirts of Moscow and emerged into featureless housing estates, with commuters picking their way to the multistorey blocks across muddy, unpaved squares. Passengers ranged from the young to the quaveringly old, all behaving well: no pungent food, no feet on seats and no litter. On the very long escalators some, mostly men, were deeply immersed in books as they rode up or down. In one crowded train, a sweet-faced elderly man with sparse white hair and a shabby old-fashioned overcoat started to offer me his seat. I smiled and thanked him but gestured that I was getting off at the next stop. He said something in reply and I'd have loved to try a conversation in whatever common language we could find, but a crowded carriage wasn't the place to identify myself as a tourist. I indicated ruefully that I was stone deaf and he tutted sympathetically.

My little burst of freedom was ending, but I looked forward to swapping city for country. The new group arrived and off we went by coach to Suzdal, a so-called 'museum town' 216 kilometres from Moscow whose thirty-odd ancient churches and monasteries had been restored and put on show. It was small and with a refreshingly rural feel, yet top-heavy with treasures – I saw far more onion domes in Suzdal than I did in Moscow – from the brooding mass of its twelfth-century Kremlin and the glitteringly opulent Cathedral of the Nativity to the endearingly simple, wooden, eighteenth-century Church of St Nicholas. I could have browsed for days.

Our sweet and rather giggly Intourist guide, Natasha, pronounced 'church' as 'khoorkh', with the 'ch' as in the Scottish 'loch'. After a couple of churches and with more to go, we gently corrected her and she giggled even more. She was proud of the 'Intourist Complex' on the edge of town where we were staying: a modern, spacious, rather characterless purpose-built place that was geared to accommodating groups.

My Moscow explorations had made me bold and I wanted a final burst of independence. I'd spotted a village a mile or so out of town which looked promising; in fact it was probably still a part of Suzdal, but split off from it by fields. After our afternoon visits, I asked Natasha to drop me in town 'for shopping' and said I'd walk back to the hotel – 'Dinner at seven thirty,' she warned me – then as the coach drove away I headed downhill to the village.

Oh the sense of freedom, striding along an unpaved country road! It was perfect. I came to a cluster of traditional wooden houses, with straggly flowers in their small gardens. Chickens scratched in the mud, cats ambled, bits of ancient farm machinery lay by the roadside. Fields stretched along a river on one side, up to Suzdal on the other. The few people around – all elderly – were unmistakably rural, bundled up in old clothes, talking across fences or tending their gardens. They returned my smiles; tourists often came to see Suzdal's treasures so I wasn't anything unusual.

There was a smell of woodsmoke and early-evening cooking. I strolled, stroked cats, admired flowers... and suddenly it was growing dark. I'd misjudged the time. To walk back to the hotel via central Suzdal was a big diversion and I felt there must be a short cut. I asked a woman for 'Intourist Complex' and she pointed along the river. Using my watch and my fingers I mimed 'How long?' and she indicated about thirty minutes. She took me to a small track, barely two feet wide, beside the river, leading away across the fields in roughly the right direction. I thanked her, she patted me comfortingly and I set off along it, the darkness deepening fast.

Soon the faint lights of the village had faded behind me and I really couldn't see. Moonlight would have been helpful but the sky was black. The path seemed to be narrowing, and my feet were hitting wiry vegetation at the sides. I assumed it was used by fishermen and worried that I might stray on to a side track that led to the river's edge. I had no idea how fast or deep the river might be – but was aware that I had no identification on me, so if I fell in and was carried downstream I'd be just a mystery corpse. And Natasha would be in terrible trouble for losing a tourist! This wasn't safe. All I could do was continue feeling my way blindly and shuffling forward, so slowly that I lost track of time.

Walking in complete darkness is like standing with your eyes shut – after a while you become dizzy. I spotted a tiny speck of light very far ahead on the opposite bank and tried to focus on it. Step shuffle... step shuffle... and then rain began to fall, heavily, smearing my spectacles and making the light flicker.

Could it get worse? Oh yes! Suddenly, ahead of me, I heard the movement of something large. Cows in the field, perhaps? Sheep? But the regularity suggested it was a person, walking towards me. The path was too narrow for two to pass so I took a step sideways into the undergrowth, not daring to go further in case there was a ditch. But he/she would still pass so close that we might touch. Should I say something? But what? Which of my six words of Russian? How on earth could I explain, in pitch dark, what I was doing there? So I started to hum, very tunelessly, the only Russian tune I could think of: the Volga Boat Song.

As he passed I said a gruff '*Graah*' of unidentifiable greeting and he (it was a man, striding along confidently) did the same. I was enormously comforted: he must have come from somewhere that I would eventually reach. Life suddenly seemed much brighter, and positively dazzling about ten minutes later when the river rounded a bend and I saw the lights of the Intourist Complex ahead. I was dried off and changed just in time to join the others as they went in to dinner, and told Natasha innocently that I'd had such a nice walk.

Now I felt invincible. One woman in our group worked for a UK organisation that helped Russian Christians, sending parcels and letters to those (for example the poet Irina Ratushinskaya) in labour camps, and lobbying hard for their release. Obviously the authorities were watching her and, doubting that they'd consider a white-haired middle-aged woman to be a potential smuggler, I asked if she wanted me to carry anything back home. In fact all she gave me was a sheet of paper with addresses, notes and some details about icons, which I tucked into my notebook. At customs she was methodically taken apart – strip-searched, and all the contents of her cases and handbag emptied out and rifled – whereas I sailed through, and gave her back her paper on the plane. I felt that the woman in the Moscow church would have been pleased.

Russia is very different today, as is Suzdal with its many new hotels, and I haven't wanted to return. I treasure all the more my memory of those shabby wooden houses in their little gardens, the kind rural faces, and the scary thrill of stumbling blindly through the darkness with the smell of the Russian countryside around me and the spring rain falling on my face.

Janice Booth's long working life includes professional stage management, archaeology, selling haberdashery in Harrods, compiling puzzle magazines, editing 25-odd Bradt guides to various countries and travelling widely. She has organised rural development in Tamil Nadu, driven Land Rovers in Timbuktu and fundraised for a Belgian charity. In 2000 she initiated and co-wrote Bradt's *Rwanda*, now in its fifth edition and still Rwanda's only dedicated English-language guidebook. She lives in Devon within sight and sound of the sea, and is contributing author of Bradt's *Slow Devon & Exmoor* and *Slow South Devon & Dartmoor*.

Up the Airy Mountain
Matthew Parris

There were three of us: Louisa (an Italian lady interpreter from Luxembourg), a male friend, and myself. I could guarantee my friend's anonymity by revealing only that he was the SDP Euro-candidate for Hampshire Central, but as he emerges from the episode with credit, he can be named: Francis Jacobs.

We had had a long day's march. Following Peru's little Rio Tigre towards its source and gaining altitude all the time, loaded down with tents and stoves and sleeping bags, we had passed through many tiny Andean villages, been mobbed by swarms of Indian children, but finally sensed, as the air grew thinner and the villages scarcer, cares lifting from our shoulders and a pleasant weariness descending.

Before dusk we reached a rather strange Indian settlement called Jajachaca. Its mud huts were mean and nobody approached but three hideous old men. They blocked our path, more than usually far-gone on coca, remnants of the leaves of which were hanging from their teeth, and begged for money. We noticed that the llamas looked in better condition than their owners. 'Probably llama-rustlers,' joked Francis.

It was getting dark so, with the village behind us and our path clinging to the edge of a high, steep gorge, we clambered down the side to the banks of the river, a hundred feet beneath. It felt enclosed, safe: and the tents were soon up, and supper on the boil.

In the fading light we thought we saw a man halted on the path above us, staring for some minutes and then moving off: but we were not much disconcerted.

Louisa was tired but by now quite thrilled with camping. Francis had offered assistance with her bedroll in that 'Happy, darling?' way they do in the movies.

Louisa retired to the tent. Francis and I stayed up a little, talking. He started telling me a funny story about his last trip to Haiti. We laughed together, lapsed into silence. Suddenly, there was a man's voice shouting. It seemed to come from the path above – high and hysterical and in no language we could understand.

I shouted back in Spanish, 'What do you want?' The response was immediate, unintelligible but enraged.

'Come down,' Francis shouted, 'and talk to us.'

That was no doubt the SDP training: a call for dialogue. For myself, I asked myself (as one always does) 'What would Mrs Thatcher do?' The answer was clear. 'Let's go for them with our penknife!' I said to Francis.

He must mentally have consulted Shirley Williams: 'No. We'd better find out how many of them there are, and whether they are armed.'

The shouting only got worse, and we realised it was in Quechua – the Indian language. We shouted back. Then it gave way to singing – of a strange, wild kind: it filled us with unease. 'We mustn't show we're worried,' Francis said. 'Let's try "John Brown's Body" in reply.' So we did – a lusty rendering.

A great rock whistled past my ear, missing me by inches and thudding into my tent. It would have put me right out of action. I shouted angrily back. More rocks and stones rained down as we ran for the cover of undergrowth.

Louisa was out of the tent by now, and terrified. We all were. There was something nightmarish about being trapped in a gorge, beneath your enemy and unable to see him. We crouched behind boulders and bushes, the river rushing behind us and rocks hailing down from the mountain face before us.

I saw that the moon was about to rise and remembered that it was a full moon. All my life I have been a little afraid of darkness. Now it seemed to be our friend. 'Quickly,' I said, 'let's get out of here. Not all together or we'll be an easy target. You go one way, Francis; you take off your white windcheater, Louisa – it's too easy to see – and follow me.'

She did. We crept from bush to bush, zigzagging out of the moonlight, up towards a stretch of path away from the shouting. We got separated from Francis and dared not call. Reaching the path, I handed Louisa the penknife and torch. 'Run back to the village. Stay there or bring help.' She hesitated, then ran.

Freed from a feeling of responsibility for anyone else, I began to enjoy myself. I wanted to size up our enemy, so scrambled a little above the path, then slid along the mountainside, in the direction of the shouting, until I reached a cockpit of boulders perched just above the source of the noise.

It was only one man! He seemed to be wearing a light-coloured poncho and was standing with his back to me, screaming at the tents and loosing off rocks. From time to time he would dance a swaying dance, holding a stone in each hand and clicking them together violently. Then he would hurl them, with some accuracy, at the campsite. He thought we were still in it. I could have surprised him by leaping on him from behind but I am not a good grappler and Louisa had the knife.

Abruptly, and to my dismay, the man stopped his noise and loped off – in the direction of the village where I had sent Louisa. Francis emerged. Should we go after her? Before we could decide we heard her coming back. She was sobbing. Her face and arms were grazed.

She had been locked out of every hut. The village had barred its doors and extinguished its lamps. She had set out back to us. Then, on the path, she had run into our enemy, who knocked her down and dragged her along the path. She had struggled free, shouting intercessions to Jesus and the Virgin Mary (which seemed to frighten him), and escaped. He had not followed.

After a hasty conference we decided we could not stay in our tents. The site was too vulnerable: what if he should come back with reinforcements? Nor could we break camp in the dark and move on. Along the path we could be an easy target. We decided to leave our tents and move our belongings up to the cockpit of boulders I had discovered above the path. There we could see without being seen. One could keep watch while the others slept. We would have the advantage of height over any assailant.

I helped Francis and Louisa with their rucksacks and sleeping bags, and installed them in our new lookout. Then I prepared to clamber back down to the tents to fetch my own things. Just as I started, I saw something moving in the moonlight, 300 yards away. It was six men approaching silently along the path from the village. I knew they could not see me and dropped back into the bushes. Louisa and Francis were in the boulders behind me. I hissed to them: 'He's coming back. Hide! There are six. They're spreading out along the path.' (silence) 'They're throwing rocks!' (silence) 'They're shouting at us. They think we're in there.' (silence) 'Fire! They're setting fire to the bushes around the camp. Let's go!'

Instinctively we ran, clambering under cover, up the mountain. We stopped to re-form, panting. At 12,000 feet, oxygen is short, and we lay there gasping for breath. In the panic, Louisa had left her rucksack at the boulders. 'Hide, and wait with Francis,' I said, 'I'll get it.' I clambered down, back to our old hideout. Flames were leaping up from the campsite towards me and I could hear shouting and see men running. Afraid of being seen, I grabbed Louisa's things and scrambled back towards the others. Where were they? At last hissed whispers brought a response from a large bush, and the three of us huddled down together.

It was no good going back to the path. One way led back to the enemy village, the other led further into the mountains with no return. The only way was up – straight up our mountainside. What we did not know was that the mountain rose to 17,000 feet. Yet the top never seemed more than 500 feet above us. So we just kept climbing. By now, the altitude was affecting us badly. The slope could only be tackled on all fours and sometimes on our stomachs. Our handholds were sharp rocks and vicious cacti which cut our hands badly. We grew shorter and shorter of breath. Louisa was the weakest so I carried her shoulder bags and Francis's rucksack, leaving Francis to help pull her up the worse parts.

We were spurred on by the sound of distant, thin whistles and shouts coming up from the valley far below. Once we looked back and saw the opposite side of the valley lit by a great red flickering glow. We realised with horror that it was the reflection of bush fires around our campsite. We heard more whistles and they seemed closer. Louisa's nerve cracked momentarily and she started to cry. I tried to comfort her.

Up and up we scrambled, breathless to the point of nausea. We didn't know it, but we had climbed nearly 3,000 feet and it was by now many hours since we had left our campsite. What was worse, the rocks were becoming steeper and what appeared to be a cliff face rose before us. To left and right was impossibly precipitous. Behind and beneath us lay the valley of bandits. Upwards was still the only way.

We caught our breath as Louisa screamed. She had momentarily lost her footing. Quickly she regained control. But in the silence that followed we heard something from the valley below. It was a thin, high song played on the *quena* – the Indian flute – distant but clear on the mountain air. We seemed to hear in it the chilling message: 'We know where you are. We have heard you. We are in no hurry.' Louisa started crying again. She and Francis were exhausted.

'You stay here,' I said, 'and look after all our stuff. I'll go on and see if I can find a way round or up this cliff.' There did seem to be a way round. I was soon alone, out of sight of the others, and climbing. Without luggage and without dependent companions, all my fear dropped away from me again, as it had while I had been shadowing the man in the poncho. I felt exhilarated and free, climbed quickly, gaining some 500 feet among the broken, rocky cliffs, dogged only by the thought that it would be hard for the others to follow. Then I came to a rock face which seemed impossible. I stared at it for a while and at the precipices to each side, then tried a couple of footholds.

There was a way up. I reckoned I had a good chance of doing it without falling, though a fall would have been fatal, but I knew the others could not make it. It was one of those ethical choices that my Moral Sciences tutor at Cambridge had told me do not occur in real life. I looked at it from all sides and followed each possible choice through to its range of possible outcomes. The last of these reflections was: 'What will I say to Francis's mother?' That was what clinched it. 'No,' I decided. 'Back you go.'

Francis and Louisa were huddled under a rock. 'We're more or less trapped,' I told them. There seemed to be little choice: we would try to sleep until first light and consider whether and how to return. A bitter wind had got up. It was too steep, and we were too tired to find anywhere sheltered or level, but I wedged myself against a cactus, wrapped in a llama-wool blanket (a souvenir), and slept. The others couldn't. They lay there, listening for sounds of attack – but all noise from the valley had ceased.

Before dawn, we clambered down the mountain. Headstrong as ever, I led Francis and Louisa over a small cliff. No-one was hurt, but Francis ripped his trousers in a rather final way, at the back. Perched 1,000 feet above our campsite, we waited for sunrise.

Agonisingly slowly, the light crept over the snowy ridge of the Andes. It appeared that our campsite was deserted. The hillside was blackened and smouldering, but the tents were still there. With sunrise, our confidence returned. We could bypass the campsite and return to the homeward track but we could not avoid the enemy village. It seemed such a waste to leave the tents behind – but what if an ambush awaited us? I decided to go down alone, ready to run at the first hint of danger. Louisa handed me the penknife.

It was difficult descending into that valley. When I reached the campsite I had to stop, momentarily, to summon the courage to search it. The rushing river drowned all other noise, so no approach could be heard. I tried to keep watch in all directions at once, while searching. The hardest thing was to go into the tents which they had tried, unsuccessfully, to burn. There was nothing and no-one there. Everyone had gone. Luckily we had kept money and documents with us. Francis and Louisa had lost little, but my rucksack was gone – sentimental value at least – with all its contents, including a book, *Cases on Civil Liberties*. I hope the bandits find it useful.

Personally I would gladly have razed their little straw huts to the ground, careless of their civil liberties.

As I called the others down, I thought I saw the disappearing silhouette of an old woman on the skyline. Anxiously, we packed the tents. There was nothing for it but to go back, and we could not avoid passing the village. I would go through first, unladen, ready to sprint, while the others observed my fate from the path.

People withdrew into their houses as I approached but nobody challenged me. Two snowy-white llamas, shampooed and backcombed, with scarlet tassels in their ears, raised their heads and stared at me with ill-grace as I passed. I signalled to the others that all was well. As they left the village, an old crone, looking like one of the witches in *Macbeth*, stepped out of the shadows and hailed them in broken Spanish.

'How are you today?' she cackled. Francis and Louisa answered that they were in less than fine spirits. 'Oh dear! What a shame! Tell me, which side of the mountain did you go up? We were wondering…' They made no reply. 'Oh well, the night is past. You are safe now. Goodbye!'

Adapted from a story originally published in The Spectator, *1984.*

Matthew Parris worked for the Foreign Office and the Conservative Research Department before serving as MP for West Derbyshire.

He now writes as a columnist and occasional travel writer for *The Times*, and in 2011 won the British Press Award for Columnist of the Year. He

broadcasts for radio and television and presents the biographical programme *Great Lives* on BBC Radio 4. His book *Inca Kola*, recounting his backpacking adventures in Peru in the 1980s, was published in 1990 and has never been out of print.

The Girl Who Washed Her Hair

Kelly Randell

There's only so much garlic one person can take. Eleven days of garlic soup, garlic bread and fried garlic with eggs would repel even the most avid fan, and we still had four days to go on our Himalayan trek, circumnavigating the eighth highest peak in the world: Manaslu. The threat of acute mountain sickness (or AMS) lurked behind our lack of culinary diversity: garlic is often quoted as a natural remedy for it. However, I'd had enough: no more soup for me. Despite this decision, our guides later insisted it wasn't my aversion to onion's malodorous cousin that ruined everything. It was my vanity.

Our trip started as most treks do: with a desk-sized foldout map and a longing to escape the travelled road. We heard Everest basecamp had become a crowd-control nightmare and found the prospect of teetering at the edge of Lukla's runway less than appealing. Annapurna seemed more akin to rambling with apple pie, so instead we chose Manaslu. It was perhaps one of the best travelling decisions ever made. Manaslu has those perfect postcard views, vast expanses of ice and rock with jagged white peaks that could puncture the sky, draped with multi-coloured prayer flags, and a fraction of the people.

It was day eleven and we were still just snatching glimpses of Manaslu's shrouded, fishtail-shaped summit through stupas and lesser hills. One of the 'cloud-makers' – peaks so high they produce enough moisture at altitude to create clouds – Manaslu is also an exceedingly beautiful tease: it's a rare treat even in October to see the summit in all her finery. But this was it, the trek's *coup de grâce*. A tiny pass at 5,160 metres etched into the face of a glacier with a name that sings: Larkya La. Tomorrow afternoon, we would be there. Nothing lay between us but a lazy day of sipping chai and a short restful night. Wake up call: 3 a.m.

On day ten we had hit our stride, so that day's four-hour trek from Samdo to Larkya Phedi, the final lodge stop before the ascent, took a seemingly effortless three-and-a-half hours. We were jubilant; it was noon at 4,460 metres, the sun was high and warm, and a rushing glacial stream flowed between the rows of wooden huts with roofs just low enough to dry clothes. How perfect for washing.

Only pants: that was my first thought. Maybe a bra. Or perhaps even my hair. A combination shampoo/conditioner Lush bar had lain forgotten and dejected at the bottom of my rucksack for six days – cold-water-only bucket showers and negative-digit nights had not been conducive to hair maintenance. But here was sun and warmth and clean water and hours of nothing to do but twiddle our thumbs... I dunked head first.

Maybe forty-five or fifty seconds of lily-scented bliss: it felt like the best thing since European toilets – and it had been weeks since we'd seen one of those. It was a devil-may-care moment that felt exhilarating until the minute it was over. Until I flipped back my head Herbal Essences style and saw a line of shocked faces gawping at me.

A fellow trekker broke the sudden silence, 'Wow, that was brave.' She sounded equally impressed and scandalised, so I towel dried quickly with a smug laugh. Then the guides descended on me.

'Your hair. You washed it. Here.'

Oh the audacity. 'Yes, and a few clothes. They'll dry in the sun – it's warm!' Though my head was becoming a bit dizzy from its icy bath.

'Very bad – very, very bad. Warm now, but not later. You'll have trouble tomorrow. No sleep tonight. At this altitude, your hair?!'

The smugness faded, replaced with a hint of sheepishness, but I still failed to see the problem. Until my hair began to freeze. In the warm sun. At 12.30 p.m.

After that, I read 'I told you so' in every glance and casual comment – from our guides as my damp hair didn't dry underneath my woolly hat; from the cook as I refused another bowl of hearty garlic soup despite assurances that 'it would help'; from the unidentified fellow midnight visitor to the loo who I almost knocked into the (now frozen) glacial stream in a fatigued daze. I endured the curses of my trekking partner as I kept him up all night with altitude-induced nightmares. It was the longest short night of my life.

I ate three bites of garlic eggs on toast at breakfast – any more and I knew I'd see it again in an hour. A light headache tapped at my temples. The symptoms were classic. From the moment we set out at 4 a.m., I knew there was a problem, but poor judgment won: I was determined to be fine. I hadn't just trekked hundreds of kilometres to miss Larkya La; I could wash my hair in arctic temperatures and carry my own absurdly heavy rucksack. I could tough it out and make that upper lip stiff. Everything was completely fine… until we were 100 metres shy of the summit.

Until coping-with-it-and-hiding-it-quite-well stumbled gracelessly into vomiting-up-my-insides-and-garlic-and-egg-breakfast, and the tilting landscape became increasingly disjointed as my sense of vertigo escalated. There was no hiding now: all of my flippant reassurances to everyone suddenly became pathetically inadequate in the shadow of thousands of metres of angular glacial ice, sans crampons, poles or equilibrium, with hours of treacherous trail before any hope of respite. The irony of having a doctor in your trekking group? There was absolutely nothing he or Diamox could do – I needed to go down, but the only way was up.

One minute and twenty-three seconds: the length of time I spent on the summit of Larkya La. Two hundred and sixty-nine hours: the time it had taken me to get there. Her prayer flags sang, but I couldn't hear them above the marching band drumming furiously behind my eyes. I trudged across the breadth of the summit and began sliding down the other side, sending our guides into a panic. I have no recollection of the spectacular views from the summit. No pictures of my triumphant conquest. Only vague clouded memories of the tattered windblown flags to prove I had even been there. It took us ten hours in total to reach the cluster of teahouses at Bimthang – painful, stressful, excruciating hours of stumble, vomit, repeat. It was supposed to take eight. I hope my group forgives me – I'm still mortified.

On the last night of the trek, as we exchanged travel stories over local beer, the doctor assured me that it wasn't washing my hair that caused the bout of altitude sickness. I smiled agreeably until another guide around the table poked my guide in the shoulder and gestured in my general direction. My guide nodded and explained something quickly in Nepali: four faces turned to me in unison, and a murmured mixture of chuckling, tutting and incredulity spread around their end of the room. The first guide whispered in English to his German client, 'She was the one. Larkya Phedi. The hair.' Ah, yes. Her.

Their advice for next time? More time? More pills? More common sense?

'More garlic, more water, less pretty.'

Ladies, take note.

Kelly Randell decided to pursue her love of travel after finishing a PhD in Anglo-Saxon, Norse and Celtic, and joined the team at Bradt Travel Guides, where she is currently a project editor. She indulges her penchant for high places as often as possible.

Cheetah Attack
Simon King

Wild cheetahs don't attack people. A full-grown cheetah is significantly more powerful than a large dog, and many times better equipped to chase and kill prey up to the size of a wildebeest. Yet a long history of persecution from man and a naturally timid disposition means that this, the fastest land animal on earth, will run in the opposite direction if confronted by even a modestly built human being.

Hand-reared cheetahs, on the other hand, can present a few problems. With the fear of man diminished there is the potential for (and examples of) cheetahs using their speed, agility and natural weapons – a set of powerful jaws, long canine teeth and razor-sharp dewclaws – to inflict significant injury on people.

This was one of many dilemmas I faced when, together with my wife Marguerite and a team of helpers from Lewa Wildlife Conservancy in Kenya, I took on the challenge of helping to hand-rear two orphaned cheetahs. From the outset, our aim was to release the brothers, whose mother had been killed by a lion, back into the wild. If this were to be successful we would have to ensure that Toki and Sambu, as they were known, were able to secure their own meals, recognise and avoid natural threats such as lions and, perhaps most importantly of all, fear man. The last criterion was the most difficult to implement. The brothers had been bottle-fed from eight weeks of age and had started their orphaned life sleeping on sofas, running on a lawn with Labrador dogs and seeing people on a daily basis. Once we took over their education we tried to keep contact with new people to an absolute minimum, discourage contact with dogs and to introduce them to their wild world gradually with the constant protection of their human guardians watching over them at a distance.

Not all of it worked. There were times when the boys would run over to see a new human being they had spotted in the distance; and their first nights sleeping alone in the bush, when they had reached an age of almost two years, were fraught with dangers like lions on the prowl or hyena packs. Bit by bit though, they learned which animals were threatening (lions) and which they could easily outrun (rhinos), and their 'bush knowledge' was such that we were able to allow them the freedom of a 50,000-acre reserve. The only remaining life lesson was to develop a fear of man, and this we orchestrated by positioning wildlife rangers, dressed in civilian clothing, in their territory. When Toki and Sambu approached, the rangers burst out of the bushes screaming, throwing sticks and clods of earth and chasing the bewildered brothers away. After a number of these 'attacks', the cheetahs became increasingly wary of contact with humans and started giving any they spotted a wide birth. All of this was desperately hard to watch, but we knew it would be essential if the boys had a chance of surviving in the wild. And this they did.

For several months after independence, they lived well and contentedly as an inseparable pair, scent-marking their territory, and finding their own food. Then disaster struck. After eating a particularly large meal of an impala they had killed, the brothers retired to a rocky outcrop to rest and spend the night. In the morning, we visited the scene to check on their whereabouts and only spotted one of the pair, the male we called Toki. His brother, Sambu, was nowhere to be seen. We had put radio collars on both before release and the signal from Sambu's led us to the awful truth: he had been killed by lions, like his mother before him. It was a tragic loss for all who had invested so much time, effort and emotional energy in his survival and release, but more importantly for his brother Toki, who now was alone and without an important ally. To give Toki a fighting chance of survival we had to break our rules of limited human contact and once again play a pivotal role in his life. After several challenging months, during which he searched fruitlessly for his brother and almost died as the result of an attack from three mature cheetah males, we decided to move him from Lewa where he had grown up, to the nearby reserve of Ol Pejeta.

Now, instead of having free rein over the entire reserve, he was introduced to his new home in a 10,000-acre enclosure that included wild herbivores as neighbours, but not, to our knowledge, any other large predators. He was able to hunt for himself, but had little chance of coming into contact with either hostile humans or other cats that might try to kill him.

It was whilst Toki was housed in this enclosure that an incident occurred that was so unlikely I, to this day, still wonder at the chances.

I received a radio call telling me that a cheetah was roaming around the outer perimeter of Toki's enclosure. I assumed he had somehow escaped and sped over in my 4x4 to try and encourage him back into the safety of the fenced area. When I arrived near the main gate, I was greeted by a small number of Conservancy Rangers, among them Steven Yasoi who had worked closely with us throughout the rearing of both Toki and Sambu and who was stationed near the enclosure. Steven immediately informed me that there was indeed a cheetah, but that he did not think it was Toki. I soon spotted the cat myself and could see at a glance that this was a stranger. It was sheltering in the shade of some cactus bushes, but I could see that, unlike Toki, it was not wearing a radio collar and it appeared to be smaller, more lightly built. After a short while this new cheetah got to its feet to find deeper shade and I could see that it was a female. It was extremely confident near the car, and indeed paid no attention whatsoever to the small group of rangers standing and talking some 100 metres away. This was odd. If this was a wild cheetah

I would have expected her to at least be staring at the men, and more likely running in the opposite direction.

This is where I made my first stupid mistake.

I assumed that this was also a hand-reared cheetah; that someone had got wind of the fact that we had a male cheetah in a large enclosure and had 'dumped' their cat on our doorstep in the hope that we would take her in. From time to time, orphan cheetahs do come into the care of humans who, with all good intentions, rear them only to find that they are very boisterous and potentially dangerous – especially around children. It is also illegal to have a cheetah in captivity without a special licence. It was not beyond the realms of plausibility that somebody had dropped their troublesome cat at the gates of this potentially good home. In all the time we had spent with Toki and his brother Sambu over the past four years, neither one of them had ever been aggressive towards us, or any other human being, and it was with this in mind I made my second very stupid mistake.

I got out of the car and decided to approach. Perhaps she would follow me into the enclosure gates, and provide Toki with a potential mate.

I walked gently towards the point where she was resting, talking to her the whole time. She turned to face me, then rose to her feet and gently walked in my direction. That clinched it for me – she must be a tame cheetah – and I spoke to her more clearly, saying (embarrassingly) 'Hello sweetie'!

I thought I heard her starting to purr – a trait uniquely reserved for cheetahs amongst Africa's big cats, and a sure sign of contentment or appeasement. But something was wrong. Her body language was shifting from a gentle walk into a head-down threat and I now could hear that the purr was in fact a low growl. And that's when all hell broke loose. She ran at me and jumped up to try and bite and claw my face and torso. I instinctively raised my right leg and planted the sole of my foot into her chest as she jumped. Her dewclaw raked at my leg and her teeth sunk briefly into my boot, but the power of the kick threw her back a little and she stood before me, growling, before sidling off towards the group of rangers who were wisely making their way back to their vehicles.

I still believed she was hand-reared – this was, I thought, the only explanation for her complete lack of fear of man. I also believed she presented a real danger to other humans, especially children, so decided to keep a close eye on her and try to mobilise a team to dart her and take her into a holding pen for closer observation. Steven followed her at a distance on foot, whilst I drove around ahead of her to try to prevent her from disappearing into thick bush country. By the time I reached the bottom of the small slope down which she had walked, she had launched an attack on Steven. I could see him struggling, with his thumb firmly grasped in her jaws. She then lunged at him, pushing him off his feet and clawing at his legs and chest. I saw red. Infuriated by the cheetah's attack on my friend, I leaped out of the car, ran to the struggling pair and grabbed the cheetah by the tail and the scruff of the neck. She turned her attention to me, and tried to twist around to bite me. Luckily my grip was firm and the worst that she could do was to rake my forearm with her sharp dewclaw before I was able to wrench her from Steven and throw her as far as I was able in the opposite direction. I yelled at Steven to get into the car and I quickly followed him before the cheetah could gather her senses and return to attack again.

A dreadful thought now began to dawn on me. This behaviour, even for a bad tempered hand-reared cheetah, was completely out of character. It was, however, in keeping with the effect rabies has on its victims. I had seen the tragic demise of hunting dogs to the ravages of rabies twenty years earlier, and shortly before their death they displayed uncharacteristic fearlessness and sporadic bouts of extreme aggression. We waited for the ranger's vehicle to join us and start tracking the cheetah before driving to a safe distance where I could tend to Steven's wounds. I also radioed for a team to arrive to dart the cat, and before very long she was sedated and housed in a cage for observation. It was possible she was indeed just stroppy, but I had to be sure.

In the meantime, Steven was rushed to the local hospital to start a course of post-exposure rabies medication. I had received a vaccine some years earlier and, though the booster was overdue, I felt that I should keep an eye on the cat before heading into the hospital.

As she roused from the effects of the sleeping drug, it was clear she was not at all well. Her eyes appeared sunken, and a white froth was forming around the corners of her mouth. She chewed wildly at a plastic water container in her holding pen and then started biting at the bars. I did not have the facility to kill her, nor would I have done so before dawn even if I had. I wanted to be sure she was not simply reacting to the confines of her enclosure. As it happens I did not need to. By dawn she was dead, a heavy froth around her gape, her pupils fully dilated. I immediately set off for hospital for my own course of post-exposure rabies medication whilst organising for the deceased cheetah's head and brain to be sent to Nairobi for autopsy and diagnosis. The results came back about a week later. She tested positive for rabies. It was a tragic end for such a beautiful cat and an incredibly rare case. Rabies is rare at the best of times and when it does appear it tends to be seen in dogs and their cousins like jackals and hyenas. Solitary cats like cheetahs have rarely been diagnosed with it.

Several years on, both Steven and I are fine. But I shall always look back at this encounter, and the string of mistakes I made in assessing the situation as a very valuable life lesson: to err on the side of caution when dealing with magnificent, but potentially dangerous wild animals, and never allow assumptions to guide actions that may lead to myself, or others around me, coming into harm's way.

Simon King OBE, naturalist, film-maker and author, was born in 1962 in Nairobi, Kenya. His love of wildlife began in Africa; his first career choice was to become an elephant when he grew up! At the age of only thirteen he teamed up with naturalist Mike Kendal to create a series of programmes  entitled *Man and Boy*, his first foray into explaining the mysteries of nature to the general public. He went on to create, film, direct and present many award-winning TV programmes and films, some of the best known being *Springwatch*, *Big Cat Diary* and the *Life* series plus more recently *African Cats for Disney*. Simon is closely involved with a variety of wildlife charities including being the current president of The Wildlife Trusts.

The Forbidden Bottle
Christina Ammon

It was never my intention to get involved in Morocco's underground drug trade. I lack a criminal disposition, and tangling with law enforcement and winding up in a foreign jail is not my idea of a thrill. It was the legal enchantments that drew me to the town of Chefchaouen: the mountains, the rivers, the blossoming almond trees.

But intention means very little in the labyrinthine medinas of Morocco. Set your GPS how you like, you'll soon find that you don't control your destiny so much as get dog-tired and wind up in situations: cornered by a guilt-wielding carpet seller, or trying on dozens of djellabas that you never even wanted and will for sure never wear.

My criminal career began over a plate of gnocchi at a tourist restaurant known as The Mantra. I try to avoid these places because they're so wrongly removed from the local culture, but after days of wandering the medina half-lost, when I found myself in front of its colourful sign written in English, I couldn't resist.

The familiarity of it was comforting. It was the off season and a difficult time to be a solo traveller. The weather was cold and the main square near empty. I'd spent the morning envying travelling couples perched together on the walls around the old mosque, sipping the country's beverage of choice – mint tea. My boyfriend, Andy, would catch up soon and although the alone time had been beneficial – I always become a poet in the quiet drift of solitude – restlessness drove me out this one day, eyes open, in search of connection.

I entered through the doors of The Mantra and a host led me to the top floor. When we crested the staircase, the room had a vague haze. Smoke. I looked for a source. Burnt chicken tagine? Incense? Did we need to call for a fire extinguisher?

'Welcome,' exhaled a man in purple pants. A plume of smoke swirled around his beard. 'Martin. From Belgium.'

Chefchaouen is famous for the marijuana – or *kief* – that thrives in the surrounding mountains. Though technically illegal, it's proffered and smoked openly and a mainstay of the rural economy. It took me a while to notice it out in plain sight – partly because I wasn't looking for it.

What I *was* looking for was a glass of wine – which holds the opposite status in Morocco: though it's technically legal, Muhammed forbids drinking in the Koran, and his word – in the minds of many – is mightier than any secular law.

I consider myself a responsible traveller, and am careful to abide by local customs. When I arrived on Morocco's shores, I had no objection to covering my arms, or respectfully removing my shoes when I entered a house. But abstaining from alcohol was more difficult. Wine, in my world view, was a crucial accompaniment to food and so no matter how delicious the tagines were, no matter how savoury the kebabs, every meal tasted of something missing and all I could focus on was the lack. Quite simply, the Prophet's belief that wine was *ummul khabais* – or the root of all evil – was ruining my meals.

In my hotel room, I perused internet forums for advice on where to score a bottle, but it seemed the closest Merlot was in Marrakech. Meanwhile, there were huge rounds of fresh local goats' cheese at the street markets just begging for a glass of *vino tinto*.

At The Mantra my wine craving had reached an intolerable peak. The menu – a tome of savoury Italian selections: bruschetta and tagliatelle, lasagne and linguine – seemed implausible without a wine list. I turned in my chair, feeling defeated.

'What's good to eat here?'

'Everything,' Martin said, exhaling another plume. Then he qualified: to be honest, it was hearsay. He couldn't afford any of it. After five years living in Chefchaouen, he'd achieved a nearly cash-free existence, living on a nearby farm and growing veggies for bartering. He just waited at The Mantra on market day to catch a ride back to the farm.

I ordered blue cheese gnocchi and looked around the room. I'd heard that owning a restaurant was as stressful as being a surgeon, but the owner Jonah, looked relaxed. While his Moroccan waiter expertly ran the show, he alternately doodled, puffed a chillum, and changed the stereo tracks from Ray Charles to John Lee Hooker. Martin would later tell me that Jonah was navigating heartbreak by smoking kief and cranking out the Bic pen drawings that papered the walls, hung mid-air from threaded mobiles, and covered the menus.

My gnocchi arrived in a clay tagine dish. I dug in and I knew it was excellent, but all I could taste was the missing Merlot. 'You want a hit off this?' Martin extended his pipe. I held up my hand: *No thanks*. The smoke-choked air alone made me high.

'What I really want is a glass of wine.'

'Good luck. This town is bone dry.'

Martin and I became friends and a few days later made plans to meet for dinner at The Mantra – my treat. But before meeting him I'd planned a three-hour hike with a self-proclaimed 'guide' name Achmed, who I'd hired in the town square. I followed Achmed up a long, wide road above town, and we stopped at the top of a mountain for the view and a cup of mint tea. Then, instead of retracing the easy trail in front of us, Achmed suggested we go over the lip of the summit.

I baulked. 'What about the time?' I asked, reminding him of my dinner meetup with Martin that evening.

He promised, 'No problem, no problem.'

Two hours later the sun was setting as we picked our way, heads down, through the slippery scree and ankle-twisting terrain on the other side of the mountain. When we at last reached the road, men in djellabas passed us with donkeys on the return route to their villages. The sky went pink and Venus blinked on, but I was too exhausted to appreciate it. The hike was supposed to be three hours. We were pushing five.

I walked with a slight limp and when we rounded a bend, the lights of town seemed impossibly far.

'Another hour,' Achmed said. I tripped in a pot-hole and began to sniffle. 'Ah Christina…' he consoled. 'Take my hand…'

And in what I can only explain now as some sort of helpless surrender setting in, I reciprocated, grasping Achmed's hand and allowing him to lead me down the mountain, strangely consoled and annoyed at the same time.

The band of light on the horizon was now a deep Cabernet. I thought of dinner with Martin at The Mantra: another wine-less Italian meal. 'Achmed,' I cried. 'I wish I could find wine in this town!'

He was eager to assist. 'This I can find for you.' My spirits brightened. My limp disappeared.

When we arrived in town, I followed Achmed around the outskirts of the medina for another mile. At last he stopped at an unmarked door. 'You go.' He stood back and motioned me forward, but my conscience tugged: *Was this really OK? Was I about to get Achmed in trouble?* But within seconds my moral hesitation was eclipsed by craving and, emboldened by the thought of gnocchi paired with wine, I pushed open the heavy wooden door.

Inside the smoky din was another world: a line of men were bellied up to the bar and drinking frothy beers. There was music and good cheer. A tall man stood behind the bar, a red light illuminating his bald head. I was astonished.

What was this pub doing in the middle of conservative Chefchaouen? I didn't know, but wasn't about to question it.

'A bottle,' I ventured.

He leaned forward. 'Red or white?'

'Red.'

He slid it into a plastic bag, which I smuggled into my canvas bag and then paid him. It was that easy.

I arrived at The Mantra late, and Martin was already up in smoke. Jonah was sitting in the same chair, transfixed by his chillum and a new Bic pen masterpiece. He OK'd the wine, so long as we kept it discreet out of respect for his staff. He pointed to a low table behind a partition and went to the kitchen to rustle up an opener.

I lowered myself on to the couch, knees throbbing and face wind-chapped. I held the contraband under the table and pulled the cork.

Martin was impressed. 'I've lived in Chefchaouen five years and had no idea...'

I ordered the gnocchi again and we toasted under the table. While he freely exhaled lungfuls of kief, I nursed my wine with discreet sips which forbidden tasted better.

Martin's conversation was as meandering as the medina, drifting from subject to subject like an aimless cloud and waylaying me in an eventual white-out. I was too tired to care whether he made sense or not. Mostly, I leaned back and felt proud of myself; I'd infiltrated the underground wine trade of Chefchaouen in five days flat and rather liked the sensation of being a criminal. The words of my friend Pat came to mind: 'If you are not a minor criminal of some sort in this day and age, you are not truly living.'

In the ensuing days, Chefchaouen would become a far more interesting place than the pretty blue-washed medina it is famous for. I developed a sort of x-ray vision, an ability to see beyond the surface of things into the dark underworld ways where animal appetites find their outlet. I saw threadbare cats pillage backstreet dumpsters and young couples kissing covertly among the cemetery tombstones on the edge of the village. I learned which boulder hideout the heroine junkies favoured, and spied a fist fight breaking in the alley just as the five-o'clock prayers sounded from the mosque.

I didn't admire the mountain town any less. After all, if I'd wanted just the pretty picture, I'd have hired an official guide, followed an itinerary, and stuck to mint tea. But Chefchaouen would have been reduced to a humdrum postcard memory: just another place where I ate chicken tagines and tried on pairs of lovely babouche slippers.

Anyway, Andy would arrive soon, and I'd have my nose out of trouble. Mischief courts only the solo traveller. I'd miss my criminal days, but be happy for the sobriety and the coherent conversation and a different sort of mischief. Until then, I had a half a bottle of wine left, a round of goats' cheese, and the sweet free sensation of having let my law-abiding, politically-correct self take a wrong turn in the labyrinthine medina of Chefchaouen, all for a glass of Merlot.

Christina Ammon's stories about wine, travel, and paragliding have appeared in *The San Francisco Chronicle, Hemispheres, Condé Nast, The Oregonian*, and many other publications. She lives in southern Oregon wine country in the U.S., but spends several  months each year living out of a biodiesel-fuelled campervan in Europe. She chronicles her adventures at www.vanabonds.com.

Trusting my Instincts
in Tanzania
Donald Greig

I t was the day before the end of the Gulf War: 26 February 1991. Iraqi troops had fled Kuwait City and George Bush (Senior) was soon to declare the hostilities over. It was too early for any ceasefire effect to reach Heathrow, though, and security there remained tighter than ever. For this particular young journalist, twenty-something and wet behind the ears, it was all just an adventure. *Trust your instincts and go with it*, I told myself. *What could possibly happen?*

Flight schedules were all over the place. In particular, my flight, Ethiopian Airlines to Arusha in the north of Tanzania, wasn't exactly going according to plan.

'Don't worry!' insisted my contact at the airline. 'When you reach Dar just go into the office in town and they will be expecting you.'

Seems straightforward enough, I figured.

'Oh and by the way, we're going to have to re-route the flight out of Heathrow.'

Re-route? Really? What sort of re-route?

Quite a big re-route as it turned out. Never has a flight plan to Tanzania been so contorted. From Heathrow to Rome to Addis Ababa. All change. Then on from Addis to Entebbe and down to Dar es Salaam, depositing me 400 miles south of where I actually wanted to be on a witheringly hot afternoon at the stale end of a fourteen-hour journey.

Dar es Salaam means 'haven of peace', but peace eluded me as I grappled with my limited Kiswahili in an effort to reach the airport's one public telephone, enticingly positioned just out of reach behind a glass partition. The phone was eventually passed to me and I managed to get through to the airline office in town, but to little avail. No flights to Arusha until the following day.

My face must have said it all for a girl behind me struck up a conversation and, perfectly demonstrating the kindness of strangers, said that I could stay the night at her parents' house. Worldly-wise as I liked to think of myself, I felt no apprehension in immediately accepting. Here was a friendly, helpful, middle-class Tanzanian girl offering a traveller a helping hand. Surely nothing untoward could happen?

We piled into a matatu van with many others and half an hour later were dropped off outside Sarah's home, a bungalow surrounded by lush gardens in a leafy, well-tended suburb. My instinct had been right. This was all going to be fine.

Sarah's mother was on the front verandah. She looked surprised when she realised her daughter was home as Sarah hadn't confirmed when she would be able to get back. She was even more surprised to see me, for Sarah had rushed back to Tanzania from visiting her boyfriend in the Middle East because her father had died unexpectedly four days earlier.

Sarah's mother was on her way to the cemetery. I was invited to go too, and a macabre sense of curiosity tempted me to say yes, but it would have been too intrusive for comfort. Their kindness at such a time was humbling. They wouldn't hear of me finding somewhere else to stay and insisted that I make myself at home until they returned.

That evening, after everyone had returned from the cemetery, in a show of what I took to be completely unnecessary generosity at such a time, Sarah's brothers insisted I join them on a tour of Dar es Salaam. What a great opportunity, I thought, a tour of the Tanzanian capital with people who knew their way around. How fortunate for me that things turned out this way. Off we went.

Their car was a low-slung affair (though it hadn't started life that way) and I felt in dire risk of injury wedged into the springless front seat, knees up to my chin, as we weaved through the back streets at breakneck speed. Eager young traveller that I was, macho camaraderie wasn't my strong point. However, with a forced grin fixed determinedly on my face I gamely joined in the wolf-whistling at the local girls, the hilarious high jinks of playing chicken with pedestrians, and the ravenous gorging on flame-grilled gristle at a roadside food stall.

I had been on the move for around twenty-four hours and my reality was beginning to blur into a sequence from a Tarantino movie, an effect which was enhanced when we pulled up outside a wreck of a building in a shabby neighbourhood of shacks, low-wattage street lighting and stray dogs. Had my instincts been quite so right after all, I wondered?

'Just stopping for a minute to see someone,' said the brothers. 'You'd better come with us; don't wait in the car.'

I followed them inside where they went straight to a door towards the end of a dimly lit corridor. I heard raised voices and held back. Then suddenly there was shoving, shouting and arguing. I peeked around the edge of the door just in time to see a fist making contact with a young man, no more than late teens. He fell heavily but within seconds was sitting upright again, proffering wads of cash towards the brothers, who grabbed the money, turned and walked out, pushing me back down the corridor in front of them.

It turned out that money lending and debt collection were a lucrative sideline for these respectable brothers from Dar es Salaam, and I had just been witness to what, by their own account, was one of their tamer transactions.

I prayed that it was time to return to the house, and to bed, but the evening wasn't yet over. One more visit was required, this time to a small shop down a narrow side street in another dodgy part of town to check on the progress of false passports that had been ordered a few days previously.

Making false passports is (as I discovered) a meticulous job which requires considerable care and expertise, and I was intrigued to meet the immaculately turned-out craftsman who operated from the back of the shop. In his mid-fifties, he had been manufacturing identities for many years and clearly took great pride in his work, though I learned later that in recent months the quality had slipped. ('He's been at it too long,' said the brothers, 'his eyesight is going.') In this particular instance, after close inspection, it was decreed that a good job had been done. Money was exchanged, passports tucked away, and we slunk off quietly.

The following morning I returned to the airport and caught a flight up to Arusha without any problem. The rest of the trip passed smoothly and I spent ten days exploring the area with a view to promoting it back in the UK. I mountain-biked in the Rift Valley, cooked with the Maasai, and even camped in the bottom of the Ngorongoro Crater. My experience in Dar had begun to dim in my memory and I was therefore unfazed when, out of the blue, I was asked by a friend of my contact in Arusha if I would carry a package back to the UK. 'Just a little package. A present for a friend.'

Warning bells should have rung. Loudly. Especially after my night in the capital. But without hesitating I said 'No problem'. Surely there had been so much mishap and mayhem for one trip already that nothing else could befall me?

On my final day I was dropped at the airport and made my way through security. The airport was small and we had to identify our baggage before it was loaded on to the plane. The security guard picked up the present box and shook it. It didn't make much of a sound. He gave me a look and I shrugged my shoulders.

'Is this yours?'

'Yes,' I replied.

'What's in it?'

'I don't know,' I said meekly, immediately realising how foolish I had been to agree to carry it.

The guard contemplated the box for a moment and then started peeling off the paper it was wrapped in. I watched, curious but nervous.

Inside the box was a wooden carving.

'Have you been given jewels?' the guard asked. 'Gemstones? Or Tanzanite? Do you have receipts?'

There followed a series of exchanges, questions and denials, all the while a crowd of fellow passengers gathering to watch and listen. Eventually, the guard tired. With a sudden smile, he waved me on.

On take-off from Arusha the pilot obligingly circled the top of Mount Kilimanjaro at 19,000 feet. It was spectacular and, as I gazed out the window, I reflected on what had been an eventful trip and on the fact that I was pleased to be heading home.

At Heathrow I collected my bags and with much purpose made for the exit. Straight through the 'Nothing to Declare' channel I headed, only to be brought up short as I was pulled over to one side to have my bags searched in what was to be the most nerve-wracking twenty minutes of my life.

'What do we have here then, sir?' they asked as they looked at the carving.

I told them it was a present. And that I had been asked to carry it. They looked at each other, then back at me – mid-twenties, slightly scruffy, backpack, just in from Tanzania – and it was obvious where this was heading.

Then they came up with a totally unforeseen and quite terrifying suggestion.

'Why don't we x-ray it and then you can be on your way?'

I paled from head to toe.

They took away the carving for x-ray. As far as I was concerned, that was it. I had been caught trafficking drugs and I was going to be banged up for a Midnight-Express-style future at her majesty's pleasure. I couldn't believe how mind-blowingly stupid I had been. What on earth had possessed me? I had always prided myself on my instincts, trusting that everything would be fine, and in a relatively lawless African capital such blind faith had been almost justified. Back in the UK, though, it was a different matter.

The customs guy returned, grim-set face.

He looked me straight in the eye and with just a hint of a smirk said, 'All clear. You can go.'

I collected my bags and, with carving in hand, headed out of the airport. My instinct was to look back over my shoulder. But I didn't.

Donald Greig first started travelling at the age of six when his family moved to Hong Kong. Since then he has visited most continents in twenty-five years of travel and wildlife writing and publishing. In 2007 he took over from Hilary Bradt as Managing Director of Bradt Travel Guides. Seven years later  he decided to return to his roots in his native Scotland and to a freelance career in all aspects of publishing, and with his partner is currently writing the new Bradt Slow Travel *Dumfries and Galloway* guide (www.slowbritain.co.uk).

The Whale
Jo Forel

He glides quite elegantly around the river bend, that great blubberish Peruvian in his little yellow pants. And though the current looks angry today, it deposits him gently on the only large flat rock available, as though planned by some great choreographer. He may or may not be breathing.

This, the latest in a surrealist series of events since our departure from Lima, comes with its own set of questions.

Is he alive? Where did he come from? And surely, if superficially, why the pants?

It becomes apparent that the answers can be found pickling themselves to pieces at the bottom of a bottle. He is, as the snatches of whippet-fast Spanish tangle in my ears, extremely drunk. And apparently a fan of swimming.

I look down from my vantage point at the frayed edge of the road, as the coachloads of Peruvians begin to shout and run and act. As they clamber into the river and haul this pisco-soaked soul out of danger and on to dry land like some brave but disorganised human crane. As he lies unconscious under a collection of donated and rainbow-hued jackets, from people who have little to give.

And it's funny, I think, because that's the thing with travelling: as soon as you get on the plane, as soon as you buckle up and accept your first glass of flat Coke from the Lego-haired hostess, you open your eyes. Really open them. You take everything in, however dull or extraordinary. Yet this man, beached on his rock, the most adventurous traveller of us all, can't see any of it.

He isn't awed by the vast open sky shining down at him, a luxury for me as a Londoner used to packing herself into a drizzling pocket of beige cloud.

He can't see those hills, green with cacti, clenching like giant grass-haired knuckles as they punch their way down to the riverbed.

At the time his eyes started to blur and his words became conjoined, he can't have known I was on the bus, a speck under a cheap polyester blanket, watching a new world through smudged windows. The clean tang of ceviche still prickling my tongue.

He has no idea that the road above him disappeared about a minute before we arrived, with just an hour left of the twenty-one hour judder to Cusco. That we gambled with the end of the rainy season, a magnet for landslides along this slender cliff of road that twists and turns like a tangled pile of hairpins.

That we weren't waiting for him to wash up, but watching the forklift painstakingly move the rocks and debating whether to give up on our coach. That the avalanche is the whole reason we're there. And that he's still here.

Worst of all, he's oblivious as the rescuers pull his friend out of the water ten minutes later, the drinking buddy who wasn't lucky enough to land on a rock. Who splutters and gasps and wraps an arm around him in childlike panic before slumping still against his chest. Before the men with sober faces come to take that friend away, a leaden form in the police blanket, hung between them like a funereal hammock.

He doesn't know he didn't make it.

We take a chance, decide to abandon the coach and its chain-smoking Scots, busy comparing bites and adventures and what they might consider a tan. I haul my lumpen backpack out of the hold and weave through the toddlers wailing in the heat, the sheep that must belong to someone and the drivers made redundant by the rocks. I clamber down, the road crumbling along with me, just trying to get to the other side, flag a car, get to Cusco.

But the river doesn't scare me now. It's him that's the worry, that slab of man who might have given up. I stumble through the weeds, smell the water as it growls past, reach him. I look. He makes a reassuring splutter and a gurgling snore. A sign that he's ready to open his eyes, come out of limbo, meet the world again. As, indeed, am I.

Jo Forel is a writer and born and bred Londoner with a penchant for jumping on planes. After graduating from Central Saint Martins and spending a decade as a creative copywriter for advertising agencies including Mother London and Saatchi & Saatchi, she went freelance, went wandering  and picked up a pen. Jo was shortlisted in the Bradt/*Independent on Sunday* Travel Writing Competition for her 2009 account of campaigning for Obama in Pennsylvania and won the Best Unpublished Writer prize in the same competition in 2013. This is her first published piece.

Jebel Marra

Nick Redmayne

'You've been in Khartoum too long,' announced Frank, flat delivery in a rural Virginia accent matching his features, adding irrefutable emphasis to his conclusion. It was 1987, I was twenty-one and had been on the run from the next instalment of my life's soap opera for several months. Arriving in a sandstorm, stepping into the night after a week's ferry and train journey from Aswan in Upper Egypt, the University of Khartoum Student House had been the cheapest gaff in town – six weeks later I was still there. Frank's accusation of semi-permanence was unsettling.

Chris, another new arrival at the student house, was a lanky English catering manager in his mid-twenties, wont to recount tales of portion control, convinced of his own superiority and in another age a shoo-in for the Colonial Service. Over individually purchased Bringi cigarettes, glasses of aromatic tea and bowls of *ful medames* beans, he convinced Frank and me to head west to Darfur and hike with him into the volcanic caldera of Sudan's Jebel Marra mountains – a remote part of Africa furthest flung from the ocean.

Chris's Boy Scout relationship with the great outdoors was far from intuitive. His knee-high woolly socks worried me too. However, he had a compass, knew how to take back bearings and possessed a skinny, yellow book by Bradt Publications entitled *The No Frills Guide to Sudan* that contained pen and ink maps of the kind used by escaping POWs – those who didn't make it. We were an unlikely trio of conflicting personalities – a Deadhead, a corporate cook and a dropout – drawn together in the dusty capital of Africa's largest country amidst the pointless tragedies of the continent's longest civil war, bound loosely by a shared desire to keep moving.

Sudanese bureaucracy, on the other hand, seemed determined that we all stay put. Sedentary clerks at the Ministry of Foreign Affairs painstakingly noted requests in blue carbon papered triplicate for necessary visa extensions, and then disappeared for a long lunch. Travel permissions, detailing names of towns and even small villages on our route, together with camera permits, both stamped on random-shaped scraps of paper, were grudgingly extracted, signed by the officer in charge and eventually flicked across desks by bored military clerks. After this paperchase, three days and a thousand miles of viscerally jarring 'bus' and truck travel to Darfur were sheer delight.

In Nyala, Darfur's regional centre, I spent a full day in the souk choosing and negotiating to buy a £1 aluminium cooking pot: a lesson in becoming too close to your subject. As we collected other necessary items for the trek – tea, biscuits, torch batteries, etc. – Chris lectured on the subject of a German hiker who'd died of thirst in the Jebel Marra crater, whilst smugly packing his own ten-litre Barnes Wallis collapsible water carrier. Frank, on the other hand, bought cigarettes, smoked and attempted to calculate how long ago he'd last drunk a beer or had sex.

A miserable night ensued on the porch of Nyala's police station, propped up against our packs, bags over our heads in an attempt to escape the attentions of the bloodsucking malarial mosquitoes from hell. The pre-dawn call to prayer was a merciful alarm that saw the mozzies clock off, only for the blowflies to clock on.

The tiny village of Menawashi was a twenty-five kilometre truck ride north of Nyala, and in the morning it was from here we started trekking. Despite lack of sleep I felt young and strong, and we were all glad to be stretching our leg muscles, intrigued by the unknown challenges ahead.

Bob Geldof had visited Jebel Marra a couple of years earlier, following the Band Aid concert. Since then scenes of the Sahel famine had become synonymous with Sudan, a waterless flyblown desert characterised by desperate, gaunt-faced adults and the distended bellies of children whose tears were only dried by thirsty flies. Which, after a couple of hours' walking, made it all the more surprising when at the neat grass hut village of Marshing we were met by a radiant, smiling woman proffering cool water and a large bowl of chicken stew. Under the shade of a purpose-built shelter we looked at each other, puzzled by her generosity, and then ate.

It was another five hours' trek to Mellem, where the yellow book promised a 'resthouse'. The landscape at this point was fairly constant, a low thorny scrub broken by a sandy track whose occasional ruts hinted at infrequent traffic. Human encounters were few. Wandering shepherds practised an elaborate sequence of polite exchanges 'giving thanks to God, 'Alhamdulillah', before asking which village we were going to, which village we'd come from and where was this village of 'Britannia' anyway? A wizened old woman, shrunken by decades of toil, a homemade blunderbuss across her back, rode up astride one of Sudan's understandably pissed-off-looking donkeys. She described a slow circuit of our company, eyeing us up and enquiring aggressively what three sorry-looking *khwadjahs* (foreigners) were doing.

'What's the incidence of donkey ride-by shooting?' enquired Frank dryly.

'I'm English,' said Chris, hoping to explain everything. In the end she gave the donkey a sharp thwack with her stick and trotted off, muttering.

At the village of Mellem a welcome party bounded out to meet us – an angry, yelping pack of yellow-eyed feral dogs. There was nowhere to run and anyway we were too weighed down and too tired. I scrabbled for a couple of handy rocks and threw one. My aim was off but the dogs were obviously familiar with the message and beat a hasty retreat.

The 'resthouse' proved a conundrum for the villagers and amongst the existing simple structures there were no obvious candidates. True to form,

Chris asked to see the 'head man' but no-one was keen to own up. In the end, after filling our water bottles, we walked beyond the range of curious children and found a piece of ground free from thorns and scorpions in which to lay our bedrolls. Sleep came easily.

Morning ablutions witnessed an unwelcome uncertainty in my digestive tract. After almost six months' rough travel this was nothing new, a common validation of being elsewhere. We packed up early and struck out on the next leg of the trek, two days' wild hiking without sight of a village. As we walked the countryside changed; almost imperceptibly we gained height. Signs of cultivation disappeared, and the track became lost amongst thickened scrub. The horizon crept closer and in places became marked by stands of trees.

Some things stayed the same; the sun was as unforgiving as ever in its attention to desiccating the soft, the succulent and the ill-prepared. My intestines were churning and halts were becoming more frequent. Surely it would pass. Replacing lost fluids, my two-litre bottle had become disturbingly light. By mid-morning Frank, to a lesser extent, was sharing my pain – it was all we could do to find different bushes. Chris's collapsible water carrier had remained empty and carefully stowed in his pack, none of us volunteering to carry extra weight. Amongst an arid landscape of thorn bushes and dry, stony ground, it was more than a minor oversight.

I lagged behind and became bizarrely trailed by a stray goat, a bleating kid separated from its herd, vainly looking to me for reassurance. A splitting headache now displaced rationale, remaining consciousness overtaken by rising feelings of nausea. Stumbling and retching, I managed a controlled collapse under the nearest substantial tree, slipping off my pack and holding my head. Frank looked as bad as I felt, sunken eyes in a sunburnt face somehow drained of vigour. He complained of hallucinations, saying he could hear a goat. Seeing the goat didn't help.

Chris had become increasingly silent, and through my malaise I recognised his concern. 'So, how much water do we have left?' he enquired matter-of-factly. After shaking our bottles, just over one-and-a-half litres between the three of us was the salutary reckoning. It was over a day's walk to the next village and the sun was still high in the sky.

Addled by fatigue, dehydration and continuing gut lurgy, desperation was creeping in. Frank had taken out his knife and was hacking at the tree's trunk. 'Some of these things store water. I read it in *National Geographic*.' I left him to it and wandered away uncertainly to 'ease myself'. My body was in revolt, vision blurred and limbs weak. It was hot, probably mid-30s but I was shivering. On the sandy ground a few feet away a vine of desert melons lay almost as though discarded. Picking one up I slit it open, hoping for some sweet, sugary flesh. Instead a dry, pulpy mush yielded disappointingly intense bitterness and little else. Back at the tree, Frank looked whiter than ever, and blood oozed from a deep cut in his thumb. 'We could kill the goat,' suggested Chris, only half joking.

We rested in the shade, by three o'clock hoisting our packs and pressing on. Though the sun's heat was diminished, the featureless plateau we traversed afforded zero cover. Footfall after footfall, in a hypnotic daze I tramped, occasionally unbalanced by thorn bush roots, strung out behind Frank and Chris. Perhaps wisely, the goat had long since chosen a different path.

My water was exhausted. In a reassuring show of humanity the others shared out what little remained of their own supplies, sombre expressions and demeanour rather than words reflecting the increasing seriousness of our situation.

Close to the Equator darkness falls quickly and as the sky showed the first ochre tones of evening we were still miles from anywhere. In the absence of signs of human activity we began to wonder if we'd taken the wrong track. There was light enough for another hour and in this gloaming we considered our situation. 'Do we walk on with torches or camp for the night?' asked Chris.

I was beaten, my spirit possibly more thoroughly crushed than my body. 'I need to rest and wait for the morning,' I confessed, not really caring to look that far ahead. We made camp.

There was no wind but uneven ground and unsettling thoughts kept sleep at bay for hours. Overhead a few familiar constellations tracked across the sky, though most were lost against a mist of normally unseen stars. Feral sounds drifted through the night air, the strangled call of jackals punctuated by undefined cracklings in the undergrowth, but most unsettling was the repeating chorus of my own deafening idiocy. The bastions of youthful indestructibility lay beside me in ruins, levelled by poor hygiene and thirst.

'Do you hear that?' said Frank. I said nothing. Chris stood up, as did Frank. I stayed prone, still awaiting a merciful end. 'There it is again. Holy shit it's a truck, there are the lights.' Crashing and squeaking across the plain, gears grinding, out of nowhere came the most beautiful beaten up four-ton truck I've ever seen. The driver, unsurprised both by our presence and our request for a lift, happily idled whilst we hauled ourselves and gear aboard. I wedged myself in, legs against a drum of diesel, soothed by the labouring engine note and the violent jostling of the ride.

Before dawn we rumbled into the sleeping market village of Dribat. I can't recall thanking the driver – though I hope I did. At a café that never really closed the owner was roused and I sucked down glass after glass of warm, sweet tea dosed with salt, and then slept.

In the proceeding hours my body quickly healed itself, while Frank too regained his strength. Over the course of the next six days we completed the trek into Jebel Marra, taking turns to shoulder the filled water carrier.

'Yes, we should all congratulate ourselves,' said Chris at the end, stiffly shaking hands.

'Didn't you think I'd make it?' asked Frank.

Over twenty-five years later I still remember Chris's response.

'I thought you'd make it. I didn't think we'd all make it.'

Nick Redmayne is a freelance reporter specialising in emerging and post-conflict destinations from North and West Africa to the Middle East and Central Asia. Recent travels have included the tumult of both Libyan and Egyptian revolutions, trekking across Tunisia's Saharan sand seas, and driving his own elderly estate car from the UK to Syria, Lebanon and Jordan. It's hardly necessary to read between the lines to understand that assignments featuring five-star all-inclusive resorts come close to his worst nightmare. Many of Nick's pieces, along with regular posts, can be found on his blog theirresponsibletraveller.co.uk.

Diving into Danger
Emma Thomson

We dip into the water like teabags, bobbing on the surface and then slowly sinking into the inky ocean as we let the air out of our BCD (buoyancy control device) jackets. All sounds become muffled as we move between worlds. Our torch beams slice through the jet-black water, picking out the plankton that streams like snow on a dark winter's eve. We are on a night dive on Holmes Reef – a submerged coral atoll marooned 125 miles east of Australia's Great Barrier Reef in the Coral Sea.

We've been moored next to this unspoiled spot for four days and haven't seen a soul – just the limitless ocean smooching the skyline in all directions. Our eight-berth boat is the only lifeline and I keep a keen eye on its anchor that morning as our diving trio – my boyfriend Bart, our new acquaintance Matt, and myself – sink slowly to the sandy floor on a daytime dive. We kneel in a semicircle next to the other six divers from our boat, cross our arms against our chests and wait. Zebra-striped damselfish and a fluorescent yellow tang, tiny lips puckered as if about to plant a kiss, swim past and blue-streak cleaner wrasse abandon their post on the rock behind me to sniff at my wetsuit-clad arms. Then, without warning, they vanish – as if a vacuum cleaner had sucked them up in one great gulp.

A shadow appears to our right and an almighty oceanic whitetip cruises into view, followed by another and another: the 'three sisters' we'd been told might appear. They command complete attention as they nose through the water displaying their massive dorsal and pectoral fins, rounded and dappled white like snow-dusted mountain peaks. They must each be over three metres long. My eyes lock on to them like missiles, hypnotised by every switch and turn. I'm not afraid, just in awe. But unimpressed by the lightly bubbling statues seated on the seafloor, they quickly retreat into the blue and we continue our dive.

Bart points cautiously to a brown-and-white cone shell partially buried in the sand – a single drop of its venom can kill twenty people – but we're distracted by a yelp from Matt who is being nipped on the legs by a territorial Picasso triggerfish. You can almost hear her clipped matronly voice scolding him like a misbehaving schoolboy. He swims upwards to escape her sharp beak, forgetting her turf is shaped like a fan, so we motion for him to swim horizontally out of her catchment and she eventually desists her chastising. Low on air, we head for the surface and take a few hours' rest to ready ourselves for the night dive.

Later, with the celestial streak of the Milky Way blazing above, we climb down the metal ladder and plop into the ebony ocean. We pull on our fins, give each other the final 'OK' signal and descend into darkness. At ten metres we reach the coral outcrop, as expected, and begin to spy on the ocean's nocturnal goings-on.

Crabs raise their claws like criminals caught in the act; parrotfish, snoozing inside self-blown mucus bubbles, hover spaceship-like just above the seabed; and a disgruntled ray shimmies out of the sand and darts into the gloom.

I see that Bart and Matt, who are swimming just ahead, have overlooked a large lobster marching along the seafloor, so I tap them on the shoulder and rub my tummy while pointing out his position. 'Dinner!' I mumble through a stream of bubbles.

We still haven't encountered any sharks, which should be out feeding. In fact, the sea is suspiciously quiet. I flicker my torch across the paths of Bart and Matt to get their attention, raise my hand vertically to my forehead – the standard diving symbol sign for a shark – and shrug my shoulders. They shrug back, also confused.

I fin closer to the rock face, trying to spot smaller species instead. Holding my breath to keep me absolutely still, I crane closer to watch a nudibranch salsa from one coral crop to another, wiggling its cerata seductively. Suddenly, a row of jagged white teeth grins into my goggles. I jolt back and the wizened face of a moray eel rears out of the rock, mouth agape and its glassy eyes staring me down. I hold my hands up apologetically and swim after the others, the drum of my heart beating louder.

Ten minutes later we happen upon a cave opening. Bart signals, with walking fingers, that he's going to check it out first and that we should follow. We wait a minute or two, then Matt signals for me to go. 'No, no, ladies first,' I gesture. He lets out a stream of bubbly laughter and swims into the hole. I focus the beam of my torch on the surrounding rocks, looking for more nudibranchs, while I wait my turn. I pan around slowly to face the open water behind me, scanning the seabed, when WHAM – a luminescent-green eye swims straight in front of me. I let out an automatic shriek of surprise, but the rubber regulator in my mouth muffles the noise. A primeval fear claws at me as I recover my grip on the torch and point it into the obsidian sea. Again, the almost-neon eyeshine appears to my right and glides past and this time I can see it's a black-tip reef shark – a big one, over two metres. Normally, this fairly docile species wouldn't bother me, but he's unusually beefy and, realising I'm over a hundred miles from land, the darkness strips me of my confidence. I keep the light trained on him and relax a little when he veers away. *The light will scare him off*, I assure myself. But then he's back: fins angled down in hunting mode this time, snout lifted as if readying for a bite, and circling closer and closer. He barges past me no further than the length of a flipper;

his wake of water pushing against my chest. And with that I abandon all composure, spin round and plunge myself into the cave, finning as fast as I can until I, unexpectedly, erupt out of the water like a champagne cork beside Bart and Matt floating on the surface. 'SHARK!' I scream, ripping my regulator out of my mouth.

'Whaaat?' they stammer. And in gasping breaths, I relay the turn of events. I wait to feel the knock against my legs – but it never comes. I jerk round to see where the boat is. The lonesome light on the top deck blinks like a saviour star 300 metres away. 'Great, just fantastic!' mutters Matt. 'We can't re-descend, so we'll have to swim back on the surface.' I flinch inwardly: we'll be more vulnerable to an attack from beneath, but I keep quiet, knowing the boys are thinking the same thing.

We roll over on to our backs – best not to see what might be below – and start finning towards the blessed boat, linking arms to make ourselves look bigger: a giant six-finned creature not to be nibbled. We talk nonsense trying to distract ourselves, but shark-attack movie scenes reel furiously in my head and I berate myself for my clichéd cowardice.

By the time we reach the boat the adrenalin has dissipated. I climb the ladder and peel the mask off my face. The boys are shouting and laughing with our bearded captain – retelling our close-shave tale – but I peer over the edge and am confronted with my reflection. *Would I have behaved differently in daylight?* I ask myself. Almost certainly. When the ocean is blue and bright, you're able to spy potential threats and move out of the way. You're calm, in control, top dog. But when blue fades to black and each fin forward is akin to an outstretched hand fumbling in the dark, you regress to a trembling pup – certain that your place on the food chain has slipped a few notches. Everything seems bigger and meaner wrapped in shadows. A good diver should keep a lid on their emotions, but I had let them run amok. Panicking had placed me in a risky situation – the thud of my accelerated heartbeat transforming me from an interesting foreign object to potential food. My overactive imagination had posed the danger, not the pearly whites of an interested shark, and I feel a fin of guilt slice through me.

Emma Thomson is an award-winning freelance travel writer and a member of the British Guild of Travel Writers. In 2012 she won the prestigious Virgin Holidays Responsible Tourism Award for best responsible travel writing and was also shortlisted for Young Travel Writer of the Year at the British Travel Press Awards. She has an uncanny ability to get into scrapes while on assignment, but enjoys the fact they make for better stories.

Take the TOTSO to Truro or Get Lost in Lostwithiel

Simon Calder

Sometimes, irresponsibility is a prescription for misery. For example, it was foolish to think (as I had prior to a trip to Borneo) *I'm sure I can find some size 11 trekking boots in Kota Kinabalu*, only to end up climbing the island's highest peak, Mount Kinabalu, wearing sandals. But a little irresponsible travel can also be serendipitous.

The essentials for any journey? A map and an open mind. On the final Friday of August, though, I set off with neither.

I was staying with friends in the Cornish fishing village of Fowey. ('Pronounced Foy to rhyme with Joy!' as the tourist people are keen to remind you.) Its pastel confusion of pretty cottages, draped over a steep hillside above a fine natural harbour, now constitute a cheerful holiday enclave. But in previous lives, Fowey has been central to many momentous journeys. For a time, it was the departure point for Celtic pilgrims sailing to Brittany for onward journeys to Rome or Santiago de Compostela. In the sixth century, St Finbar stopped here on his way from Ireland to Rome, and his pilgrimage is commemorated in the name of the village church, St Fimbarrus. A millennium later, the ship *Frances of Fowey* sailed with Admiral Frobisher in search of the Northwest Passage; Cornishmen found themselves in the frozen wilderness of Baffin Island.

My journey on that breezy day was slightly less adventurous: I was trying to get to Truro, Cornwall's county town. BBC Radio Four had invited me to take part in a programme. However, there is not a decent studio-quality connection to be had within a twenty-mile radius of Fowey. So I agreed to cycle over the hills to the railway station at Par and catch a train to Truro, home to BBC Cornwall.

There was, I thought, no need for a map: I had biked in the opposite direction from the station a few days earlier. But as I pedalled unsteadily up Lostwithiel Street from the waterside, my mind was not as open as it might have been, because of an email I had received that morning.

'I've now reached crunch-time regarding the final contributor list for our fortieth anniversary title, *The Irresponsible Traveller*,' it read. 'The cover designer is starting work on Tuesday and he needs a list of contributors to feature in the artwork.'

The author of the message was Adrian Phillips, Managing Director for Bradt Guides. He had kindly asked me to contribute to this book. But I had already written up the 'Mount Kinabalu in sandals' episode for *The Independent*, and so needed to come up with a new example of peripatetic irresponsibility. That issue was preoccupying me as I puffed up an absurd gradient. And while I pondered, I missed the TOTSO.

I have never owned a car, but I like to think that decades of hitchhiking have acquainted me with the inner workings of Britain's road system. A TOTSO, as you perhaps know, is a junction where you are proceeding along a particular route but you have to 'Turn Off To Stay On' due to the design of the junction or orientation of the roads. In northeast Kent, for example, the A2/A299 junction is a TOTSO. Going east, if you fail to turn off to stay on the A2, you end up in Margate rather than Canterbury or Dover.

Coming out of Fowey, there is a tiny TOTSO at the head of the village. At a roundabout, you have to turn left to stay on the main road to Par. But with my mind focused on Adrian's urgent message, I did the natural thing and cycled blithely straight ahead.

The road soon settled into a lovely Cornish lilt through the hills. On one downhill stretch, I gazed around to seize the joy of the moment of late summer in Britain. And that's when I realised I'd not TOTSO'd.

To my left, I should have been seeing the chalk downs crumbling into the Channel. Instead, the sturdy spine of Cornwall was rising, while the land to my right fell away towards the valley of the River Fowey. I was going north, not west.

I could have cursed, turned around, retraced my tyre tracks to the roundabout and taken the correct exit. That would have been the responsible course of action. But I decided to keep going on into the map-free unknown. I knew that at some point I would reach the Great Western railway line between Paddington and Penzance, and speculated that it would cross the River Fowey in Lostwithiel. I plan rail journeys with some sense of self-responsibility, so I always aim for the departure before the very last train I can safely catch. That meant I had a bit of time in hand to reach Truro and the studio.

After a few more sinew-stretching rises, I hit the A390. I swung right along the main road for southern Cornwall and freewheeled into Lostwithiel. The welcome sign distilled its history and appeal into a series of increasingly strident fonts. 'Ancient Stannary Town,' read the first line, referring to its role as home to the Stannary Parliament, looking after the interests of tinners. 'Charter 1189' was followed by 'Twinned with Pleyber Christ – France,' referring to its Breton sibling. The biggest letters, though, were reserved for a 21st-century message to hard-pressed visiting motorists: 'FREE PARKING'. I was too keen to reach the station to pay much attention to these many attributes, but the gentle muddle of Georgian townhouses and ecclesiastical remnants intrigued me. I pedalled across the medieval bridge to the station, and bought a day return to Truro. A local train resembling a garden shed on steel wheels rattled in and rumbled along to the county town just in time for the interview.

On the train back, I met a man sipping from a can of beer and wearing a T-shirt with a slogan reading 'For my next magic trick I'll need a condom and a volunteer'. He got off at Par. Tempted by the earlier glimpse of Lostwithiel, though, I stayed on for an extra ten minutes to my starting point.

At the municipal museum, housed in the Corn Exchange and adjacent Town Gaol, I learned that the name Lostwithiel derives from the old Cornish expression for 'The Town at the Tail End of the Forest'. It is a fine language that can encompass that within four lyrical syllables. Since the thirteenth century Lostwithiel has been the lowest bridging point over the River Fowey – the nine-arch structure over which I had cycled from the station. The economic geography made Lostwithiel the natural choice as hub of the tin and China clay industries – and, for a time, the capital of Cornwall. The decaying Duchy Palace testifies to declining fortunes. While the River Fowey is tidal as far upriver as Lostwithiel, it silted up and the town lost business and significance.

The museum chronicles civic misfortunes, with exhibits such as an 1853 poster warning of the risk of cholera. 'There should be no division in the citadel when the enemy is at the gates... Every accumulation of offensive material is a pestiferous battery... You are blessed with a constant supply of pure water... Remove your nuisances, willingly.'

I don't think I was being a nuisance, but I removed myself, willingly, by cycling up Skiddery Hill past a series of sturdy stone cottages in search of a pretty way back to Fowey.

Cornwall's natural good looks make it tricky to find a way that is not pretty. My basic chart-free plan was to stick to the west side of the meandering river, climbing and descending according to the ancient lanes that lace the terrain. I funnelled through an arch of geriatric trees on a track worn deep by time, then emerged to the wide-open countryside just as a summer shower of monsoonal proportions began (irresponsibly, I had no wet-weather gear). But the wheat fields, woodland and hedgerows still looked lovely. Afternoon in late August is when England is at her ripest.

Simon Calder

A small act of human kindness arrived in the shape of a tray of marrow and rhubarb. 'Help yourselves. Donations invited for Cancer Macmillan,' read a sign on a garden gate. Then on along an ancient lane that carved a furrow through the county.

As I rode, the centuries piled up on either side of the lane. The cutting drilled beneath a railway bridge. Nothing odd there: Cornwall is fretted with old lines that were closed down during the cull in the sixties. Except this one appeared to be far from derelict, with working signals and assorted cautions from Network Rail. But I knew Fowey no longer had passenger trains, which is why my irresponsible bike ride had been necessary.

'To the church (XIIIth century),' gestured a signpost outside the riverside village of Golant. The stone was the colour of storm clouds, the churchyard full of Celtic crosses and gravestones whose inscriptions had been erased by time. The old village library, a handsome, high-roofed hall, was emblazoned 'Reading Room'.

The road along the river, named Water's Edge, carried a useful reminder that it might flood at high tide. But the fishing craft and pleasure boats would lie impotent on the mud for a few more hours.

'Golant Down is the way to go,' I was assured by a local when I asked for directions that did not involve getting my tyres wet. He pointed me to a pathway that threaded up over the southern shoulder of the village. It was not cycling territory – it was better than that. Wild flowers illuminated a fern-fringed pathway that trickled towards the sea, converging with the Saints' Way – the freshly signposted old pilgrimage route from Padstow on Cornwall's north coast. Close by stood a seventeenth-century watermill converted into an upmarket recording studio and used by the likes of Robert Plant and Oasis, but as the day dwindled, birdsong provided the only soundtrack.

By this stage I was dragging my bike through the undergrowth. Fowey could surely be only a step away. Suddenly a familiar sound in unusual circumstances cut through my ruminations: the raucous blast of a locomotive's horn. A freight train rumbled into vision, its cargo of China clay destined for foreign potters. Absurdly, Fowey is connected to the national railway network but only for freight rather than passengers – or 'self-loading cargo' as we are sometimes disparagingly known. I passed the old station on the northern fringe of Fowey, then threaded through the dainty shops and twee cottages (special mention for you, Baggywrinkle). Thanks to a mix of incompetence and good fortune, I had enjoyed a fine adventure. And furthermore I now had an answer for Adrian Phillips of Bradt. Next morning, I could write: 'Yes, I have a tale of irresponsible travel I can contribute to the book. I remember it as though it were yesterday. That's because it was yesterday...'

Simon Calder has been travel correspondent of *The Independent* since 1994, and is now the owner of Ordnance Survey Explorer sheet 107, 1:25,000 covering St Austell, Liskeard, Fowey, Looe and Lostwithiel.